George Henry Calvert

Brief Essays and Brevities

George Henry Calvert
Brief Essays and Brevities
ISBN/EAN: 9783743349803
Manufactured in Europe, USA, Canada, Australia, Japa
Cover: Foto ©ninafisch / pixelio.de

Manufactured and distributed by brebook publishing software (www.brebook.com)

George Henry Calvert

Brief Essays and Brevities

BRIEF ESSAYS

AND

BREVITIES

BRIEF ESSAYS

AND

BREVITIES

BY
GEORGE H. CALVERT

BOSTON:
LEE AND SHEPARD, PUBLISHERS.
NEW YORK:
LEE, SHEPARD AND DILLINGHAM.
1874.

Entered, according to Act of Congress, in the year 1874, by
GEORGE H. CALVERT,
In the Office of the Librarian of Congress, at Washington.

RIVERSIDE, CAMBRIDGE:
STERROTYPED AND PRINTED BY
H. O. HOUGHTON AND COMPANY.

CONTENTS.

ESSAYS.

I. EARTHLINGS	9
II. LADYHOOD	12
III. GENIUS AND TALENT	17
IV. ARISTOCRACY	22
V. ORGANIZATION	29
VI. WORK	35
VII. SOCIAL PALACE AT GUISE	42
VIII. WORLDLINESS	49
IX. ART	55
X. TRAVEL	61
XI. OBEDIENCE	70
XII. FREEDOM	73
XIII. THE BRAIN	78
XIV. MATERIALISM	90
XV. THE LIFE TO COME	96
XVI. BOOKS FOR BOYS	106
XVII. F. W. ROBINSON	115
XVIII. GOETHE'S FAUST	123
XIX. SHELLEY	129
XX. SHAKESPEARE	140
XXI. THE MERCHANT OF VENICE	149

XXII.	Taming of the Shrew	.	.	.	.	.	154
XXIII.	The Tempest	.	.	.	.	.	157
XXIV.	Macbeth	.	.	.	.	.	167
XXV.	Hamlet	.	.	.	.	.	177

BREVITIES.

I.	Spiritual, Moral	.	.	.	.	.	193
II.	Literary, Æsthetical	.	.	.	.	.	208
III.	Conduct, Manners	.	.	.	.	.	239
IV.	Miscellaneous	.	.	.	.	.	255

BRIEF ESSAYS.

BRIEF ESSAYS.

EARTHLINGS.

When one has just spent an hour in a police court or the "Tombs," or reads of the diversified daily crimes by countless criminals, or dipping personally into Wall Street, feels himself a party to the selfish scramble which makes up so much of life, or tries to count the lies that are sneaking or buzzing about, or thinks of the manifold rascalities, rampant or covert, and the multiform sensualities that darken and deform humanity,—one might, in certain moods, be misled to believe that man is, after all, but a low, creeping slave, the dupe of vulgar desires and ignoble impulses, a restless, insatiable earthling. Earthling though he be, his eye carries his thought up to stars whose light has been thousands of years in reaching him; and there, his inward vision dazzled with the transcendent grandeur of creation, he is at once humbled and exalted; and humility and exaltation both attest a higher than a mere earthly being.

Within his magnetic brain are other chambers, built to be opened to deeper meditation, to be illuminated by still finer light. "Only by celestial observations can terrestrial charts be constructed," says Jean Paul. In man there is an upper heavenly sphere; only by help of this can be instituted and conducted an orderly human life. Unguided, untempered by these nobler capacities, even the lower could not accomplish their specific functions. Here is the celestial canopy which gives amplitude and security to man's being. The vaulting sweep of disinterested feeling, open to men, constitutes their humanity, their divine humanity. Without the breadth and freedom of this upper range, men were not men, but a herd of low-cropping bipeds. Take from a man his capacity to be just, to be charitable, to bound up from the very depths of despair upon ever-surging waves of hope, to feel at times a thrill shoot through him from Infinitude, — cut him off from all this, and you discrown him, you disorb him. By no intellectual projection, by no scientific dexterity, can he be launched and upheld on his proper path. Only the power of trustful intuition, of a sure moral sensibility, can lift and hold him to his human track. Destroy this power, and he flounders in the mire of animalism. A more appalling sight could not be than a scientific animal, a being endowed only with impulse and full intellect. And think (if the imagination can stretch itself to such an abstraction) of a tribe of such: I do not say community, for community there could not be, that implying an organized combination for the general good; and where men were purely selfish, there could be no permanent combination, no tenacious apportionment. Think of a crowd of Calibans and sons of Mephistopheles: nay, a crowd even of such miscreations could not be. Either, they would fly asunder by mutual repulsion, or assail each other's being ruthlessly and destructively. But the beauty and grandeur of the divine scheme exclude such monsters. In the worst specimens of our kind, in a Nero or a Borgia, there stirs the germ of the generic and noble. Through the darkest and coldest nature penetrates somewhat of the light from a holy internal fire. Did there not, the individual would shiver and burst in his own icy darkness. Pure black cannot be.

II.

LADYHOOD.

EXAMPLES of ladyhood should not be sought in the Sultan's seraglio; for ladyhood implies independence of spirit and womanly self-respect, with ableness for self-direction; nor would one look for the higher illustrations in a community coarse and unfashioned; for ladyhood is an emanation from the heart, subtilized by culture. Nor would you be likely to come upon the finer type among the rings of the garish, bedizened, recurrent whirl of fashion; for a continued blaze of publicity is no more favorable to the growth of ladyhood than is gas-light to the ripening of rose-buds. Ladies of the purest water hesitate not to enter Broadway, but they neither seek nor enjoy an ostentatious thoroughfare. The glare of its gaze, if too often submitted to, dries the auroral moisture which glistens on the countenance of ladyhood, — aye, glistens when years have pinched the smoothness of outward beauty.

Only through example and authority can the

lady be unfolded. The earthly angel or girlhood is matronly womanhood, ever hovering near its trust. Youth, permitted to be unbound and irreverent, runs into excesses, which sap its chasteness and its strength. Of adolescence maturity is the guardian appointed by nature; and nature ever punishes with imprisonment a breach of her mandates. The guardianship of matrons over girls is the guardianship of their freedom; and freedom not thus guarded, carries a latent chain in its temporary license.

Any, even the slightest, decrement of modesty lays a weight upon the spring of ladyhood, whose essence is a refined womanly self-consciousness. Nature's choicest product is woman; and modesty being the interior fount that suffuses her with spiritual bloom, ladyhood, as the consummate flower, the florescent acme, of womanhood, a distillation from its superlatives, draws from this fount a perennial freshness. Thence, the wealthiest dower wherewith a maiden can enter womanhood is modest reserve. From this deep, clear, sparkling source are recruited all the feminine virtues of her life. We say modest reserve; for there is a cold and a proud reserve, and these are barren. Modesty implies warmth, and a living store of power; denotes impulses, emotions, desires, to be directed, protected, controlled; and reserve betokens capacity to protect and control this palpitating material of conduct.

> "All integrants of being, the low and higher,
> The lords of work, the visionary powers,
> Leap with the lightnings of a holier fire,"

in a woman whose speech and bearing are ever thus guarded. A lady of the highest type is the unmatched

> "Delight of whate'er lives and wills and loves,
> The central majesty to all that moves;"

and to be this, her life must be steadied, refreshed, empowered by modest reserve.

Does it seem that in estimating ladyhood I set too much store by purity and continence, the wardens of a treasure whose unspeakable value is only revealed by what is missed when it is lost. Whoever called a *lorette* a lady? Among the richest in physical beauty and in wit she may be, with generosity even of heart; but so poor is she spiritually, there is none will do her reverence. Fallen from her height of womanhood, none now looks up to her. She has forfeited her eminence, and lives without honor, without command, without obedience. She is scarcely a person, is become almost a thing. Her being is blind with the gloom of self-destruction. The threads wherewith is woven the exquisite veil of ladyhood — a veil protective, which is a transparent beautifier — must themselves be wrought of cleanest material, their delicate fineness proceeding from their strength, and their strength from their purity. Not an outward gauze, not a super-added screen is this veil; it is self-spun, inly woven, a spiritual lacework, only traceable in the flush of its twinkle, the subtlest of magnetic auras, permeating and illuminating with delicate light the finer fibres of conduct.

If the nest wherein ladyhood is hatched be modesty, out of beauty, spiritual beauty, are wrought the wings wherewith it soars to its serene dominance. Of the higher type of ladyhood may always be said what Steele said of Lady Elizabeth Hastings, that "unaffected freedom and conscious innocence gave her the attendance of the graces in all her actions." At its highest, ladyhood implies a spirituality made manifest in poetic grace. From the lady there exhales a subtler magnetism. Unconsciously she circles herself with an atmosphere of unruffled strength, which, to those who come into it, gives confidence and repose. Within her influence the diffident grow self-possessed, the impudent are checked, the inconsiderate admonished; even the rude are constrained to be mannerly, and the refined are perfected; all spelled unawares by the charm of the flexible dignity, the commanding gentleness, the thorough womanliness of her look, speech, and demeanor. A sway is this purely spiritual. Every sway, every legitimate, every enduring, sway is spiritual, a regnancy of light over obscurity, of right over brutality. The only real gains we ever make are spiritual gains, — a further subjection of the gross to the incorporal, of body to soul, of the animal to the human. The finest, the most characteristic acts of a lady involve a spiritual ascension, a going out of herself. In her being and bearing, patience, benignity, generosity, are the graces that give shape to the virtues of truthfulness. In the radiant reality of ladyhood the artificial and the conventional are naught. Different from, opposite to, the superpositions of art, or the dictates of mode, is the culture of the innate, the unfolding of the living; as different as the glow of health is from the cosmetic stain that would counterfeit its tint.

III.

GENIUS AND TALENT.

CRUDEN's and Mrs. Cowden Clarke's "Concordances" show that in the Bible the word *genius* is never found, the word *talent* only as a measure of money; and that in Shakespeare *genius* (occurring but seven times) stands for guardian spirit or what is akin, and of the fourteen times that *talent* is read, ten are in "Timon," being there always used in the ancient Athenian sense, as a standard of money-value. In the prolific Elizabethan period, and for some time later, these two words had not set themselves into the important positions they have since held in the language. Important we call them, for the two express so much of the inward mysterious power, and the varied aptitudes of the human mind, that their suppression now were a laming of habitual utterance. Hence their so frequent use in criticism and conversation, and hence the endeavor of critics and æstheticians to define the meaning of each, and to distinguish the one from the other.

Genius is of the soul, talent of the understanding. Genius is warm, talent is passionless. Without genius there is no intuition, no inspiration; without talent, no execution. Genius is interior, talent exterior; hence genius is productive, talent accumulative. Genius invents, talent accomplishes. Genius gives the substance; talent works it up under the eye, or, rather, under the feeling of genius. Genius is emotional, talent intellectual; hence genius is creative, and talent instrumental. Genius has insight, talent only outsight. Genius is always calm, reserved, self-centred; talent is often bustling, officious, confident. Genius gives the impulse and aim as well as the illumination, talent the means and implements. Genius, in short, is the central, finer essence of the mind, the self-lighted fire, the intuitional gift. Talent gathers and shapes and applies what genius forges. Talent is ever approaching, and yet never reaches, that point whence genius starts. Genius is often entirely right, and is never wholly wrong; talent is never wholly right. Genius avails itself of all the capabilities of talent, appropriates to itself what suits and helps it. Talent can appropriate to itself nothing; for it has not the inward heat that can fuse all material, and assimilate all food, to convert it into blood; this only genius can do. Goethe was a man of genius and, at the same time, of immense and varied talents; and no contemporary profited so much as ne did by all the knowledges and discoveries and accumulations made by others. For full success the two, genius and talent, should co-exist in one mind in balanced proportions, as they did in Goethe's, so that they can play smoothly together in effective combination. In Walking Stewart, says De Quincey, genius was out of all proportion to talent, and thus wanted an organ for manifesting itself.

The work of the world, even the higher ranges, being done by talent, talent, backed by industry, is sure to achieve outward success. Commonplace is the smooth road on which are borne the freights that supply the daily needs of life. Genius, to be sure, as the originator of all appliances and aids and motions and improvements, is the parent of what is to-day common, of all that talent has turned to practical account; but genius, when it first exhibits itself, is as alarming and hateful to talent and routine as the first locomotives were to the drivers and horses of the mail-coach. Even on the highest plane of literature, the poetical, talent wins laurels more readily, and at first more abundantly, than genius. Scott and Moore were, by their contemporaries, much more valued as poets than Wordsworth and Coleridge. Scott and Moore were men of genius, but of far less genial insight than Wordsworth and Coleridge, and with more literary talent. Hence they were accessible to the many, and were by the semicritics, men of mere talent, like Jeffrey and Gifford, absolutely as well as relatively overrated. Their genius gives liveliness to the commonplaces of feeling and adventure, a sheen to surfaces that were otherwise dull; but their pages lack the sparkle that issues out of recesses suddenly illuminated by imaginative collisions, a subtle, joyful blaze flashing up from new marriages between thought and sentiment, — marriages that can only be consecrated by the high priests of thought, and which stand forever inviolate, and forever productive, in the best verse of Keats and Shelley.

Genius involves a more than usual susceptibility to divine promptings, a delicacy in spiritual auscultation, a quick obedience to the invisible helmsman; and these high superiorities imply fineness and fullness of organization. The man of genius is subject, says Joubert, to "transport, or rather rapture, of mind." In this exalted state he has glimpses of truths, beauties, principles, laws, that are new revelations, and bring additions to human power. Goethe might have been thinking of Kepler, when he said, "Genius is that power of man which by thought and action gives laws and rules;" and Coleridge of Milton when he wrote, "The ultimate end of genius is ideal;" and Hegel may have had Michael Angelo in his mind when, in one of his chapters on the plastic arts, he affirms that "talent cannot do its part fully without the animation (*Beseelung*), the besouling, of genius." Schiller concludes an apostrophe to Columbus with these lines:—

"Trust to the guiding GOD, follow the silent sea:
   Were not yet there the shore, 'twould now rise from the wave;
For nature is to genius linked eternally,
   And ever will perform the promise genius gave."

IV.

ARISTOCRACY.

ASPIRATION is a universal instinct. Vines ever strive to lay hold of what will help them to climb. Forest oaks vie with each other which shall ascend highest into the light and air. The mineral aspires toward the vegetable, the vegetable toward the animal kingdom. From zoöphyte to man each type is, at its best, a "mute prophecy" of the one above it. Upward, upward, is an innate impulse of whatever lives. All being struggles to ascend, thereby to better itself, for every mounted degree is a gain of freedom, and freedom, the highest aim of life, is the gauge of advancement. The tree is freer than the rock, and the bird that builds in its boughs is freer than the tree, and man is freer than any other animal, and his freedom is in precise proportion to the degree that the animal in him is subordinated to the human; and among individual men, as among nations, elevation, relative and absolute, is in the ratio of freedom, — the freest man approximating, while yet on the earth to the emancipated condition of the angels.

In the political and the social spheres the mounting instinct is ever active, and more diffused and lively now than in any past generation is this activity, because, since our independence and the French Revolution, there is in Christendom more freedom of movement than at any previous stage of history. *La carrière ouverte aux talents* is not a windy boast ; it is a transforming, vivifying reality, whereby France, as a state, has been for thirty years much more of an aristocracy than ever before; that is, in her political administration she has had more of her stronger men than she had under the kings and nobles who for centuries were her sole governors. Hereditary governors, one or many, are pseudo-aristocrats. Nature says to man : Choose ye for rulers the best I furnish, but do not dare encroach on my large function by aiming to confine the virtues and faculties of rulership to a few families. This is, with man's shallow devices, to try to overrule the deep laws of nature. Disastrous are all these attempts ; for not only does Nature in her breadth and justice, discountenance such monopoly, but in maturing her best specimens she exhausts the particular stock, so that the descendants of a great man are mostly like the parings and fragments of a feast, the potency of nature culminating in the one glorious product, the juices of the stock whence she drew it being by so deep a draught exhausted. Hence it is that the English "nobility" has been more of an aristocracy than the "noblesse" of France or that of other continental nations. It has not been so counter to nature; it has not been a *caste;* it has sucked at the breast of the mighty multitude. Less pure in blood heraldically, its blood is richer, more prolific, essentially more aristocratic. Take from England her Wolseys, and Burleighs, and Bacons, and Cromwells, and Somersets, and Clives, and Nelsons, and Pitts, and Foxes, and Cannings, and Peels, all plebeians, and you unman her history. Had not the blood of her hereditary rulers been thus refreshed and invigorated, her De Veres, and Tudors, and Percys, and Nevilles, and Howards would not have been so powerful and so famous. It is the virtue of the English polity, or of the English character, that under monarchic and oligarchic forms, high and highest places are kept open to the men fittest for regency, nature's aristocrats, drawn often from the lower strata of the social pile.

For its prosperous administration and endurance a republic has especial need of nature's aristocrats, of the best men engendered in its bosom. For a republic stands and thrives on self-government, and self-government can only draw its breath of life from character. Among the citizens of a large modern republic, if it is to last, there must be prevalent that union of good intentions with intelligence which results in common sense; and common sense demands of the members of a republic or democracy that in choosing administrators, they know who are the best citizens, and have the will to take them. Thus a republic, for its welfare, should be able not only to breed capable, honest men, nature's aristocrats, but, having bred them, be so alive to noble interests as to put them into its high places. In a word, a republic, to thrive, should be a democratic aristocracy, which is the same as to say it should be ruled by its best heads. Elections should be wise selections. A man without faith in humanity, or one with vision bounded to self-seeking goals, or one constitutionally despondent, might readily despair of our republic on reviewing the men who, in the past decade or two, have made and administered laws at Washington. For a score of years we have been going from bad to worse; and unless we have reached the worst, unless by an inward motion (part instinctive, part conscious) we soon swing ourselves up out of the rapacious rankness, the mercenary filth, which from staining our garments is beginning to infect our pores with its poison; unless we delegate our vast sovereign power to better men, to larger men, to freer men, that is, to men less the slaves of self-seeking, — unless, in short, we soon reverse our movement and ascend vigorously into a lighter, purer air, the tremors of the despondent and the faithless will shape themselves into the fears of the thoughtful and the hopeful, and these will have to look deeper than political forms and principles for the means of keeping the higher interests of a great people from being sacrificed to the lower, and of counteracting the demoralizing influence of narrow egotisms and a general relaxing materialism.

History teaches that artificial, nominal aristocracies run to despotism or uphold it; and that whenever a state has thriven, under whatever form, monarchical, oligarchical, or republican, it has thriven through the agency of genuine aristocracy, that is, through having its best men at the political helm.

In the social sphere aspiration is still more lively and pertinacious. Here refinement furnishes the wings for ascent. In the long run those individuals and breeds most open to impressions of the beautiful, and thence most capable of culture, form the nucleus and are the stamina of social superiorities. From this class (when social conditions have some freedom of play) accretions are ever a-making to supply the losses incurred by forfeiture of inherited social position, — forfeiture through lack of sensibilities to value and retain a polish, through lack of manly bottom to maintain a gentlemanly conduct and carriage, of delicacy to appreciate beauties of bearing, subtleties of demeanor. As in the political, so in the social sphere, there are assumptions, pretensions, audacious usurpations, and especially there are the oligarchic impudences of fashion to mar and weaken; but what is real and pure, what is truly aristocratic, what is the best socially, is a projection beyond the limited self into a sphere of æsthetic association. "Good society," if it be not an arrogated name, not vulgarized by ostentatious ambitions, but if it be essentially good, is, like art, an issue out of the finer sensibilities. It is the flowering of the social tree, not a mere fragile ornament on the top, and gracefully embodies the essence of that which it surmounts, carrying in its folds the seed for reproduction.

In an advanced civilization the desire for social preferment vibrates through the whole frame of a people. The late Dr. Bowditch, the eminent mathematician, used to tell a story of a serving-maid who related how her engagement had been broken off through objections made by the friends of her lover to the position of herself and her family. "Why, Lucy," said the doctor, "I did not know that you had an aristocracy in your class." "Aristocracy!" rejoined Lucy,' "we have more down there than you have up here." The masses, it has been said, have the sense of the ideal. Had they it not, there would be no great poets, for these are a subtle distillation out of the juices that give life and character to the mind of a people. The aristocracy "up here" owes much of its quality to the quality of the aristocracy "down there."

V.

ORGANIZATION.

THE ecclesiastical and military institutions of the Middle Ages grew out of the latent capacities of European manhood. They were protective shells wrought out of man's instincts for the safety of his body and of his soul. Clumsily were they wrought: so was astrology; but had there been no star-ward need that first vented itself in creating astrology, the grandeurs and uses of astronomy would to us have never been revealed. The military apparatus enabled civil and industrial organization to form and strengthen. The Church did similarly for the mind, giving to thought a channel, and thus saving it, in dark ignorant times, from running loose on wide surfaces, where it could have neither depth nor current, and would have tended to wayward expansion, and thence to wasting evaporation. These institutions denoted in the European population power of development and self-protection. Among the inhabitants of tropical Asia and

Africa are no such beginnings: these feel little inward motion towards, and have not capacities for, graduated outward arrangement. They never shape themselves into organic wholes; they are little more than aggregations of shiftless individualities; and hence they do not emerge into civilization. The need of, and capacity for, organization are the mark of mental breadth and resources.

To secure enjoyment and growth, the mind, with help of its executive constituent, intellect, builds for its behoof artificial structures, to shelter and further its activities. Being artificial, man-made, these structures are temporary. Even the natural body, which is God-made for the individualization of soul, is temporary, quickly mortal. Organizations, devised by human intellect, are become obstructions, usurpations, when they cease to be auxiliary to the strength and play of the higher mental powers, for whose service they first arose. In man-made organizations there is an inherent tendency to materiality, to grossness; and a sign it is that they have become material and gross, when they are no longer subordinated to the spiritual, but would govern and bound it, when they have become end instead of means, masters instead of servants. Such the ecclesiastical institutions of Europe had become in the thirteenth, fourteenth, and fifteenth centuries. Men were imprisoned in the Church. The mind, the light of manhood, the creative core, the source of life and worth, the mind was weakened, maimed, blindfolded, was thwarted and smitten by the very institution designed to enlarge and second it; as though a citadel should come to be controlled by its own outworks, as though a parent were bound and scourged by his own children. But the same inward force that first promoted the organization stirred to rend it, now that it had grown worldly and tyrannical. Many were the voices raised in protest, and many were the martyrs of freedom ; some of them like Wickliffe and Huss and Savonarola, so full of light that they still throw light on our path. At last from the heart of Germany came a voice stronger and clearer than any yet heard, the voice of Luther. This giant rent in twain the huge fabric of Roman ecclesiastical domination. How broad was the rent, how irreconcilably hostile were the two camps into which his manly might had split Christendom, Luther himself was hardly aware. More grandly and far more deeply than he knew, Luther was the assertor and spokesman of mental independence. Thenceforward one-half, and the stronger half of the Christian world, was open to free organization.

The largest, the most prolific right that man has ever achieved is the right of private judgment. In the beginning it was a protest of the free against the despotic, of the spiritual against the mechanical and material; and it insures the final triumph of the free and spiritual in all provinces of human being and endeavor. For in the right of private judgment is involved the power to exercise it, and the successful exercise implies capacity for, nay, possession of, social and political organization; and the higher this is the more complicated will it be. Note the simplicity and one-sidedness of life under despotic governments in all ages and continents, and then the diversity and the many-sidedness of American republican life. A distinctive feature of our country is the number of associations, combinations, institutions, which, originating in the wants, desires, aspirations of free self-governing citizens, grow up spontaneously, and maintain themselves within, but independent of, the State, so many *imperia in Imperio*. Hardly any day's newspaper but has a report of the proceedings of some Temperance, Odd Fellows, Woman's Rights, Free Trade, Methodist, Baptist, or other Sectarian meeting, Benevolent, Artistic, or Scientific society, — all private organizations, started for the purpose of cultivating and propagating, each one certain special principles and practices, each one nourishing some tissue of our manifold life, and all therefore contributing more or less to the general weal. These many and diverse voluntary organizations contain the essence of political self-direction : they are the healthy offspring of free spirit and free life : they temper the hardening forms of legislative rule : they lie beneath constitutions, and upheave them with their spiritual force. Besides these there are countless industrial combinations for furthering especial objects of capital or labor. All, whatever their aim or amplitude, are so many nests of self-government, forestalling much of the work of public political authority, and are at once the evidence of, and a school for, self-direction and practical self-culture, a result and a support of manly life and political freedom.

The further you go east the fewer there are of these voluntary public-spirited associations. England, next to ourselves, has the most of them. In France, under the shallow despot, Louis Napoleon, they were not allowed to be, while they are springing up in Italy and Spain and Germany, since these nations have begun their regeneration.

VI.

WORK.

We live by work; we prosper by work; we rise by work. Men take rank according to the work they do. Luther and Shakespeare are ruling sovereigns among men by virtue of the vastness and excellence of their work. All history, all civilization, is the product of work. We advance by its inventions, we thrive on its accumulations. Intellect is the parent of work; the more method there is in work, the more effective it is. The simplest garden is laid out in beds; if you sow squash, and peas, and beets, and celery, and Brussels sprouts, all together, you will have a horticultural chaos and no vegetables. Foresight, intelligence in work, are the guage of progress. Mankind rests on work, moves on work; stop work, and New York, London, Berlin, collapse. London, New York, Berlin, are great workshops.

Walk through the thoroughfares of these workshops, to learn what wealth they turn out daily, then pass into other quarters, into dark, damp, crowded cellars, and hungry attics, and reeking tenement-houses, to learn how squalor and poverty cling to the sides of wealth and luxury, like a "mildewed ear blasting its wholesome brother." A busy city may be likened to a huge monster, its upper members glittering in gold and diamonds, while its lower are bound with rags oozing with festered sores. And is not he a social monster, the single individual who, with a million in his pocket, walks through a crowd of the half-clad and the half-fed? or are not they the monsters, beings unnatural, by the side of comfortable opulence, prodigies in the face of healthy Nature?

Can this yawning chasm be filled? The pale, stooping woman in that bare, chill garret, stitching from daybreak till midnight to earn poor clothes and poorer meals, can she be brought near to that other woman in jewels and laces, who in cushioned coach is rolling to the fashionable ball, striving to turn night into day in search of amusement? They are both of American birth, possibly cousins, and both are immortal souls. Both, in different forms, are victims of conditions whose cold, pitiless arbitrariness may, within a decade, banish the daughter of the bejewelled one to the garret of the overworked and underfed. What political economist, with his formulas and superficial expedients, dares confront the vast lowering problem of capital and labor? Political economy deals with producers and consumers, not with throbbing men. Until you deal with men primarily as men, you will solve no such problems.

Individual men, and aggregates of men in communities and nations, are set in motion by, are agitated by, nay, have their very being in, feeling. Feeling propels the intellect, which is but its tool; feeling is the father of all wants, originates all work. The needs of conjoined beings, co-working for mutual help, these create society, gradually promoting it, according to the power and purity of feeling, from savagery through barbarism up to the highest levels yet attained in the more advanced communities of the most civilized nations. In the best of these, even in foremost personages, there is nevertheless but partial play given to the feelings. Hence discontents, restlessness, vice, unhappiness, despondency; and in those outwardly and personally less favored, misery, despair, crime. Free play, not to say full play, to the deep, infinitely varied, ceaseless motions of the feelings, those regents of life, those constituents of the substance of human being, free play to these demands a far closer mental association among men than has yet taken place. As human relations now are, each one does, comparatively with what he might do, little for himself, because he does and can do so little for others; it is an everlasting principle that the more we do for others the more we do for ourselves.

Men in all positions stand in too hostile attitudes one towards another. Every man is trying to get the better of somebody. There is far too much counter-working and not enough co-working. The stronger and shrewder make the many work for the few — the few growing rich, the many keeping poor. The problem of wages, the relations between buyer and seller, between producer and consumer, the reciprocal rights of capitalist and laborer, beneath all these problems, within them, above them, lie the *rights of man*, not rights political, but those rights which grow out of, inhere in, his organic nature. Now the faculties, powers, impulses, aspirations which, because they involve these rights, constitute the human being, these carry within them laws implanted there to solve all such problems, — laws, obscure it may be, difficult to discover, as laws of large comprehensiveness are apt to be. Electricity played round and through the air and earth in the days of Socrates and Cicero; and how many centuries had mankind to wait for the Franklin and the Morse to seize its law, and turn it to great uses? A deep law, covering a wide field of being or action, is ever freighted with important and with beneficent solutions.

Of deep, fruitful, social laws, Fourier professes to be the discoverer. I am not aware that any other social reformer and thinker puts forward a like pretension. At the same time without some such discovery — discovery of synthetic, far-stretching law — no solution of social and industrial problems can be reached. Is Fourier a discoverer? In recent discussions the name of Fourier occasionally comes up; in most cases to be briefly dismissed as that of a communist, free lovist, at best an impractical dreamer. Fourier is nothing of all this, be he a genuine discoverer or not. Of a thoughtful and conscientious nature, by the frauds he witnessed, and was obliged to be a party to, in trade, he was, as a young man, driven to meditate on the means of introducing justice into the dealings among men; and the result, after years of observation and study, was, that by higher methods work may be made more thorough, more productive, and, instead of being in most cases irksome, and in many repulsive, be attractive and enjoyable.

See that shoemaker, bent over his last all day, and that tailor, plying the needle eight or ten hours daily, each bound to his one task from week to week, from year to year, through a long work-weary life? Such in its monotony and irksomeness, is the life of the tens of millions of workers. Those two stout intelligent young men are capable of several kinds of work, and how willingly would each shift his hands, some hours every day, from the one endless routine to other production. There is not a sound man but is capable of more than one kind of work, many men are capable of several kinds, and some of many kinds. Figure to yourself a thousand people living in convenient proximity — not the close and foul proximity of the tenement-house — so ordering a dozen different forms of work that they could in parties of ten or twenty alternate every two or three hours, each choosing departments for which he has aptitude or liking. Here, besides the enlivening changes, they have the exhilaration of congenial companionship.

Add to this that in most kinds of work, men, women, and children are united in cheerful rivalry, and does not the attractiveness and joyousness of such work shine upon you? It is only higher organization, profounder method applied to work, whereby to satisfy, as they never have been satisfied, the wants of the human being. In this there is nothing destructive, nothing subversive. It is a change similar to that which a man makes when he sells his house, puts the proceeds into a joint-stock company, and betakes him to a boarding-house,—similar, but far more serviceable. It will be an expansion, a liberation of the worker, a change which will be justified, nay, it is demanded, by the whole diversified capability of man; is invigorating to his intellect as it will be purifying to his heart.

Let the thoughtful, sympathetic men, whose minds are now busy with the momentous questions of poverty and crime, of wages and competition, of coöperation and labor, let them give an intelligent and a dispassionate examination to the pretensions of Fourier as a discoverer of social and industrial laws. Latent in humanity there are such laws; bring them to light, and the way is opened to great solutions.

VII.

THE SOCIAL PALACE AT GUISE.

At Guise, a small town in the northeastern part of France, on the Oise, half-way between Paris and Brussels, has arisen an industrial and social phenomenon, in the shape of a human hive of busy, well-housed, well-fed men, women, and children, literally a Social Palace. Above the destitutions and squalors and starvations of the laboring masses of Christendom, this pile rears itself like an illuminated dome lighting up the dim domains of an unhealthy dream-land. But the buildings and business of this pile are the opposite of dream-like; they are the logical outcome of generations of healthy aspiring effort, the legitimate offspring of centuries of deep gestation. They stand there now a great new fact, smiling with a noble pride, glistening with hope to the civilized world. But what is the Social Palace at Guise?

In the first quarter of the present century, into the mind of a French boy, while seated on the benches of a crowded, misused school, came the wish to better its conditions. Soon this thoughtful sympathy was transferred from his school-fellows to mechanical laborers; and between the ages of eleven and twelve he set himself earnestly to work in his father's iron work-shop, that he might get command of a wide field for usefulness. As he grew towards manhood the injustices, oppressions, hardships, which press upon the toiling masses wrought on him more deeply, and set him to devising plans for their remedy. Intelligent, zealous, punctual, young Godin was early able to start for himself, and to prosper. The capital acquired by his foresight and industry he used to fulfill the broad, generous desires of his opening years; from his own high, pecuniary vantage-ground he sought to bring more justice into the relations between labor and capital, and bringing more justice, to bring greater profit to both. His is one of those clear, sympathetic natures that will not let the man forget the great dreams of the youth.

Studying in search of the best method to compass his noble wish; examining the various plans projected for associating on deeper principles the workman and his employer,

M. Godin accepted the deductions of Fourier's great synthetic mind. His own mind is of the same "large composition" as Fourier's — one of those rare organizations which combine high, strong, forecasting intellect with the bountiful sensibilities which, besides making the intellect penetrative, send the man out of himself to accomplish his dearest wishes.

The sound principle, that workmen should receive a justly proportioned share in the net produce of their work, this did not satisfy M. Godin. His plan embraced, in addition, the intellectual and social improvement of them and theirs through a unitary building. So soon as he had gathered capital enough he collected all his workmen and their families under one roof, or rather, under three roofs, a central building and two large wings, all connected together, each one of the three four stories high, with a court in the centre of each, and galleries running round the interior of the court. Near to these are separate buildings for nurseries, school-rooms, restaurant, markets, bakery, etc.; and further off are the various structures for the manufacture of stoves, this being the business of M. Godin.

Economy, convenience, cleanliness, healthfulness, cheerfulness, these are the primary gains of the unitary building. In the bulky volume of M. Godin, published in 1871, entitled "Solutions Sociales," wherein he expounds his whole theory and aims and practice, the final chapter is devoted to the Social Palace he has established at Guise. This chapter has forty-four sections. Space fails us here to illustrate the many and various advantages of such a palatial home; but from the titles of some of these sections the reader can judge of their contents and import: "Character of the Social Abode; Peculiarities of Architectural Unity; Facility of Relations; Domestic Economy; Ventilation and General Salubrity; Temperature and Heating; Absence of Insects; Water and Baths; Light, the Symbol of Progress; Light in the Day; Light at Night; Order and Tranquillity; Personal Security; Medical Attendance; Integral Education; Nurseries; Schools; Principles of Organization; Order and Liberty."

In the three connected buildings, called by their wise founder the *Familistère*, are lodged nine hundred people. Out of their share of the profits from the manufactory, food, lodging, and clothing are paid for, all to be had at wholesale prices, and of good quality. Their general interests are under the charge of a council of twenty-four, twelve of either sex, chosen by the whole body of adult inmates. Out of the common fund their children, from infancy to youth, are educated as they can be nowhere else, all the nurses as well as the teachers in the ascending classes, holding their places through their attraction to those places.

This is a great step from wages and the isolated household; and it is the initiatory movement to a higher step, which will be taken when work shall be organized under a yet deeper and broader principle, divulged by Fourier through his discovery of the law of groups and series. Work will then be brought within the scope of the prolific, beneficent sway of attraction, and of affectional sympathies. Work is the regent of all human relations; work has raised us from barbarism to civilization; every achievement is begotten, every joy enlivened, every liberty won, every virtue perfected by work. When in its many, its infinite modifications, work through thorough intellectual and affective coöperation, shall have become grateful, aye, and delightful, then will the sunshine of life tingle in all the countless hearts that now throb in the shadow of poverty, or beat heavily under the gloom of vice. In work made attractive, there is salvation, moral as well as industrial salvation. Have, therefore, no fear for morals. With increased well-being and cleanliness, with the independence and freedom gained through steady, willing occupation, is engendered a more solid self-respect, a deeper sense of personal responsibility, and thence a healthier moral tone. A sparkle there will be of mental as well as of bodily health unknown elsewhere. To life will be imparted a fresh momentum and cheerfulness, and unprecedented liveliness and honesty. A thousand people of all ages and both sexes, held together by joyful co-work — and nothing else could hold them — cannot but be sound, and the more and more sound according as greater play be given to all their faculties of intellect and feeling through varied occupation. Put the same thousand into the same building to live in idleness, unknit together by active co-working, and they would fly asunder in less than a year, scattered and shattered by discords and sensuality. When we see the effects of passions seduced and perverted, as they are now so often seen, we exclaim with awe, "How fearfully we are made!" When we shall see them all healthily active, we shall exclaim with ecstacy, "How beautifully, how divinely we are made!"

Already in M. Godin's establishment the moral tone is much raised above what prevails among the same class of workmen out of the *Familistère*. If it is still far from the highest, this is because, through the limitation of the faculties to one or two employments, freedom is limited. Moral perception grows clearer and clearer through more and more freedom. Freedom grows through the unfolding and culture of all the faculties, those of feeling as well as those of intellect; and this full unfolding and culture can only take place through intimate, variegated co-working of age, manhood, womanhood, youth, and childhood.

VIII.

WORLDLINESS.

THAT the world should be full of worldliness seems as right as that a stream should be full of water, or a living body of blood. So should a healthy mind be full of religion; yet, for a thousand years a religious man meant the inmate of a monastery, and means so now where monkery still glooms. The first equivalent your French dictionary will give you for the noun *religieux* is *friar*.

A worldling is not a man filled with the deeper, cleaner realities, delighting in what is highest and best in God's world; he is not a freeman of Nature's guild, but of man's; and thence so laden is he with the begilt and the temporary, that he has little strength for the solid and the eternal.

Within the majestic evolution of power and beauty, the incessant corruscation of God's world, before the eyes of man,—in the midst of this boundless, infinite, untangled interlacement of wheeling, illumined circles, there moves another world, dependent on, subordinate to, this primal mighty one, and sometimes obstructive of it; this is man's world, which, from a twig, has grown to be a far-spreading forest, so umbrageous at times that it is often a darkening screen between man's vision and the superior creation whence its life is drawn. From crude impulses, from few simple desires, has come, through the unfolding of intelligence, and the culture of feeling, a complex overgrowth of wants and fruitions, of arts and refinements, of inventions and auxiliaries, of discoveries and institutions, which so busy and concern, so flatter and engross civilized man, that he, their creator, has grown to be their dependent; and, limiting his life to the round of their dwarfish gyrations, converting conveniences into essentials, luxuries into blessings, things secondary into things cardinal, he in many cases is become such a slave to circumstance, so much a creature towards his own creation, that he has almost ceased to feel himself an issue of God. Many a man, many an educated man, is but dimly conscious that he is the inhabitant of an upper world. He knows of no uses but the prosaic; the sun is his lamp, the summer his gardener. Like the cloth he wears or the carriage that carries him, he is grown to be an artificial instead of a natural product. Allegiance to the divine has been forfeited; he is the obsequious burgher of a sensuous, earthly subcreation; he is a worldling.

In one of his weird, significant tales, Hawthorne writes: " Wealth is the golden essence of the outward world, embodying almost everything that exists beyond the limits of the soul." When, therefore, we say that the worldling is always a mammonist, that gold is his chief god, we draw the widest circumference that encloses his active being. His centre has not the heat to project the radii of life beyond material circumscriptions. The worldling does not live in his soul; he tries to ignore his inmost self; his habitation is on the outskirts of beautiful being. Thence he has but slight relations with the souls of other men. Living in and on externalities, the superficial is the element he thrives in; but, as the less food has of nutritious substance the larger must be the quantity taken, he, for his contentment, needs to be ever busy with the external. The internal repels him, profundities confound him; tell him he is a spirit, and you sadden him. He delights in select crowds, in showy equipages, in fashionable dinner-parties, in the glare of chandeliers. When not in "company" he is preparing for it and thinking of it. When alone, he has on his cordial expression only when he is about to go out; the putting on of his dress-coat lights up his countenance. But this is only the modish worldling, your drawing-room loafer or leader, your company-man whose diplomas are his invitations, whose rent-roll is his visiting-list. Worldliness were not worth a paragraph in a printed page, did it not busy and impel brains to which those of a dressy metropolitan gossip were but as the fizz of a holiday rocket to the flash of a minie rifle. Erasmus was a worldling, and a higher than he, Bacon, much of the wisdom of whose great essays is worldly wisdom. Napoleon was the chief of worldlings, the Lucifer of this multitudinous heaven-banished crew. Herein Louis Napoleon is very like his uncle. The high places in the State, and alas! in the Church, are apt to be held by worldlings, these having a simian talent for climbing, a prehensile gift, and sinuousness in seizing and winding themselves among the branches of the glistening smooth-barked tree that has its root deep in the soil of matter, and bears a bifold fruit of gold and power. But man can never get entirely rid of his conscience, nor smother utterly the inner self; and so, worldliness has an instinct of hypocrisy, and is ever seeking to wrap itself in veils and teguments that hide its ugliness without hampering its action ; and for this it finds often effectual the badges and tools of the highest functions, secretly hugging itself behind the gown judicial, the cloth clerical, and the rostrum philanthropical.

This falseness of aim, this exaggeration of the transient and the artificial, this deference to wealth and contempt of material poverty, this all for *having* and naught for *being*, this restless shallow activity, to which truly belong the words Burke untruly applied to all human effort, "What shadows we are, what shadows we pursue!" this unhealthiness of desire, this futile turning of the means into the end, all this, which is but a many-sided sign of the one hollowness, this protean worldliness, confining itself to no class or condition, taints members of all, from the king to the beggar, but dyes with its most gaudy stains that class in which gold most ministers to superfluity, the class which it attires as its choice victim, the class thus characterized by the spiritual, intellectual F. W. Robertson: "If you wish to know what hollowness and heartlessness are, you must seek for them in the world of light, elegant, superficial fashion, where frivolity has turned the heart into a rock-bed of selfishness. Say what men will of the heartlessness of trade, it is nothing compared with the heartlessness of fashion. Say what they will of the atheism of science, it is nothing to the atheism of that round of pleasure in which the heart lives; dead while it lives."

IX.

ART.

From the heroic combat at Thermopylæ to the simplest individualities of doing or suffering that give to the present hour its animation, every fact, event, conjunction, has its life and especial significance. To seize this life, in anything like its essential being and import, the rays shed on it from the witnessing mind must be well fed with vigor and sympathy. To him who can read them, the world is full of meanings, of hints, full of appeals. Nature is lavish of jets that issue from her glowing core, and await a spark from some human thought to flash into delightful illumination. The mind that is to ignite these jets must itself be warm with the fire of ideas. We see with ideas: he who has the brightest and clearest, sees best and farthest.

Thus vivid, the mind builds within itself fabrics of thought. Out of intuitions and of knowledge acquired it forms images, and holds and carries them in its invisible grasp. This mental power of interior construction is called imagination, and is the most intense exertion of intellect at its highest degree of action, exercised most effectually in such direction as the predominant faculties of the individual prompt. To the mercantile combiner, to the military strategist, to the measurer of stars, imagination, or the power of mental construction, is as needful as to the poet. The astronomer too, and the strategist must, in order to do their work, be able to carry in the mind combinations and completed plans. The far-seeing masterly man of business, who brings order out of a chaos of affairs, partakes with the poet of the creative power. The difference between them is, that the Poet or Artist always makes appeal to the feelings. So do the melodramatist and the prosaic novelist. But these work superficially, for rapid transitory effects. Not from a deep store of rich sensibilities are their materials drawn; for, if so, in their work would be the foundations and promise of poetry; nor, when their sensibilities are used by the imagination in fiction, are they sublimated by the supreme, by what may be called the creative sensibility, that to the beautiful; for that were the fulfillment of a poetic promise.

Poetry, Art (for Art is not Art unless it be poetical) is creative. The Artist is a creator, or he is naught; that is, the light thrown from his mind upon an object or scene, whether real or mentally constructed, must win from that object or scene a new aspect, endue it with new life, enliven it with new meaning. Poetic genius vitalizes with its own spirit what it takes in hand, and it takes a subject in hand because it can so re-animate and elevate it. It is the power and privilege of genius to be fresh on trite themes, original on old ground. Genuine Art always spiritualizes, in its means as well as its end subordinating the physical to the mental, the animal to the psychical. It appeals to the feelings in such a way as not superficially to please them or to flatter them, but in such a way as shall rejoice, and through that rejoicing, purify them. The crowning faculty, — crowning a pyramid of abilities, — which empowers the Artist to do this, is his sensibility to the beautiful, what may be called his glorifying faculty. Hence the Artist is not a copyist, a sensuous imitator of Nature, a mere reflector; his brain is not a daguerreotype plate to be painted on by the sun's rays. He is his own sun, and prints on an object fresh lines that make it a new picture. By experience, by contemplation of Nature, his susceptive mind is, to be sure, ever enriched. As Wordsworth says : —

> "From Nature and her overflowing soul
> I had received so much that all my thoughts
> Were steeped in feeling."

That he be so enriched the wealth of his æsthetic endowment must be refined by his delight in the beautiful. Within him there throbs more feeling than he needs for his every day individual use, and the superflux he throws out in products having in them so much that they live for generations, imparting life to others, like the sun who from his abounding bosom projects warm globes to animate space.

Under poetic impulse the Artist throws him out of and above his common self up to a purer, freer plane, where his vision is so penetrative, so elective, as to bring before him what is most choice. Life is full of wonders, is all wonder ; and it is the Artist's privilege to be in closer *rapport* with the divine essence out of which springs this manifold wonder ; and thence, become originative, he breathes into his work some of the breath from the creative spirit. To the grand and mysterious and beautiful in

Nature his soul gives a livelier echo, and thus is he able to make his work, as Goethe says, "seem at once natural and supernatural." The only faithful reporter and interpreter of Nature is the poetic reporter. No object, whether in Nature, or feigned in harmony therewith by the imagination, can be fully, distinctly seen, except by the light that flares higher and brighter in him than in others, the light of the beautiful. Not the most gifted can reproduce the whole, can reveal the full secret; the genial hand can tell enough to give stimulating intimations, visionary glimpses of much that is untold. Yet in itself a work of Art should not be vague or indecisive; a finite whole in one sense, it so speaks to the soul as to let us feel that it comes out of the Infinite, and it points us thither

Art, then, is a projection out of the inmost of gifted, poetic-minded men. Its source is given, quite unsconsciously, in a few lines of Raphael's letter to his friend, Count Baldassare Castiglione: "As to the Galatea," he writes, "I should hold myself to be a great Master were only half of the great things in 't that your excellency writes to me. In your words, however, I find proof of the love you bear me. Let me here say to you that, in order to paint a beautiful female figure, I should have to see many, and, moreover, under the condition that your excellency stood near me, to choose the most beautiful. But as a right judgment is as rare as is a beautiful woman, *I make use of a certain idea which springs up in my mind.* Whether or not this possesses artistic excellence I know not, *but I strive to compass it.*" The brains of Raphaels and Leonardos and Phidiases, these are the nests, high and lonely like the eagle's, overlooking the plains below, whence issues winged Art. A visionary realm is that of Art, too ethereal to be but partially incarnated; and this is its source,— a longing for, an inward mounting towards, perfection, a striving after beautiful possibilities. Art is an iris-hued transfiguration of plodding prosaic life, a rainbow everlastingly spanning the storm-drenched world.

X.

TRAVEL.

WOULD you make the most of a capable youth? Drive him away from home, even should his home be a vast metropolis, a London, a Paris, a New York. If he never quits it he gets withered and localized into a cockney or a *badaud*. A youth of mental force, especially one with the boldness of genius, will not wait to be driven. Travel is a lively educator; it opens, it expands, it liberates the mind. Observe those citizens — of the better class socalled — who never go beyond their county or state; they get to be so self-complacent about petty home-possessions, so intellectually (and unconsciously) emaciated, from ever breathing the same close mental air, so redolent of provincial egotism, that the sole self-defense their friends have is to laugh outright at such childish limitation.

When a competent man travels, he goes out of himself, he projects him beyond the narrow circle of home-activities and customary influences; his faculties by being freed, are strengthened. To go out of one's self, to forget one's self, is morally the most gainful movement that can be made. Akin to this is the intellectual liberation by travel, which, like the moral, is often rich in wide-spread benefit. Had Shakespeare not travelled up to London, what would have become of us? We should have had no Lear, no Tempest, no Hamlet, no Imogen. Stratford-on-Avon, with neighboring Warwick, could not have fed the brain out of which were to spring these wonders and giants. Much of circumstance genius can overcome; such conquest is one of its functions; but it must have room for the free play of its sprightly brood. Who will pretend that if Raphael had been born and bred in picture-banning Constantinople, the world would have been replenished with his Madonnas? Goethe was impelled to travel away from prosaic Frankfort, and his long life in genial Weimar he freshened and indoctrinated by travel into France, into Switzerland, into Italy. The best thing that Franklin ever did for himself was to run away from Boston when a boy. A new city with new influences wrought freshly on his self-reliance and resources, and unfolded his mental means more decisively. His remarkable individuality he brought with him from his birthplace, but its full development was due to his abode in Philadelphia. Travel to England completed Franklin's early self-education.

One of Milton's biographers, Sir Egerton Brydges, a genial tory, thinks that Milton's journey to Italy in his twenty-ninth year was "the preservative of Milton's poetical genius against his political adoptions." Certain it is, that what he saw and heard and learnt and felt in Italy, was a phasis in his culture which nothing else could have supplied. This journey Milton shortened, being ashamed, as he says, to remain abroad enjoying himself, while his countrymen were fighting for freedom at home. For twenty years politics withdrew him from poetry. When he returned from Italy Milton was thirty-one. Dante was thirty-six when banished from Florence. Had he been recalled after a year or two, he would, with his fiery temperament, have thrown himself again upon the sea of Italian politics at that stormy period, and the calm, abstracted moods, needed for high poetry, would not have been found. To Dante's enforced travel for the last twenty years of his life the world probably owes one of the great epics of literature.

Of single journeys the most momentous was that of Luther to Rome. In after life he declared, "I would not for a hundred thousand florins not have seen Rome, not have seen Rome, not have seen Rome. I should have been troubled for fear that I did the Pope injustice." The opening of such eyes on what they saw in Rome, and on the way thither, was an effect of travel which in turn became a cause as potent and prolific as any that human insight can trace.

A restless yearning often drives men of creative power abroad to enlarge themselves, to feast their hungry faculties on variety. Homer and Plato and Pythagoras were great travellers. Æschylus did part of his travel as a soldier, and won the crown of preëminent bravery at Marathon and again at Salamis. Socrates went on three military expeditions, two of them into remote Thrace. Demosthenes liked travel; so did Cicero and Virgil and Horace. Nor should we forget the saints, Augustin and Jerome and Chrysostom and Thomas Aquinas. To Montaigne and Cervantes travel was a harvest; and so it was to Montesquieu, Voltaire, Rousseau, to Wordsworth, Coleridge, Byron, Shelley.

The most majestic and far-seeing of travellers was Columbus. He travelled in search of a World and found it. Three centuries later, while yet the natives roamed on the hither side of the Alleghanies, there grew up in this new world a boy, who, taking on himself at the age of sixteen the engagements of manhood, started on his travels, an authorized surveyor, towards the wilds of the Shenandoah and the mountains beyond, training his courageous eye among untamed Indians, inuring his heroic limbs to toil and storm, thus unconsciously educating himself for the great journey he was, in mature manhood, to make from Cambridge in Massachusetts to Yorktown in Virginia; a journey which lasted about six years, and the fruits whereof may be judged by this, that in one hundred years from the day he started on that journey in 1776, the three millions of colonists whose national independence was secured by the capture of Cornwallis at Yorktown, will have grown to be a Republic of more than forty millions of souls, the most prosperous and most progressive nation, the most enlightened and most influential on the globe. A few years after the capture of Cornwallis, the first President of the new republic granted at Philadelphia an audience to a young French traveller, then unknown, Chateaubriand, who, in his memoirs written half a century later, thus records the interview: "Happy am I that the looks of Washington fell on me. I felt myself warmed by them for the rest of my life."

Alexander, Cæsar, Napoleon were terrible travellers. With such retinue did they move, that not only were they secure against being robbed, but were strong enough to rob and sack at any of the stations of their numerous journeys. But to humanity even more eventful than these, are another class, who may be called travellers paramount, namely Tribes, Hordes, Peoples. Under a sway resistless, and deeper than any conscious impulse, do they stretch forward on their long endless journeyings. Think of the first wave which, far back in the dim dawn of time, started westward, rolling on, we know not how far and how fast, pushed forward by stronger waves, and these again urged onward by still stronger, until, out of the vast, mysterious Asiatic womb, the whole of Europe was peopled even to its westwardmost islands. Think of those huge tidal waves, irresistible, overwhelming, which, under the names of Goths, Suevi, Lombards, Burgundians, Vandals, swept over the Roman Empire in the early centuries of our era, overlaying an exhausted population with fresh deposits of human breeds, wherefrom were to spring the modern nations of Europe, out of barbarian grossness emerging self-crowned with Literature and Art, and finally with the greatest of civilizers, Science.

Onward, still onward they again rolled, in the tempestuous track of the bold God-driven Columbus. And now, while this new World is yet but sparsely peopled, already have the stoutest of them pushed across our wide continent, and are heaping themselves up on its western shore, preparing to roll still westward on the long, broad paths of the Pacific.

Seeing what we have seen, and knowing on stronger authority than that of Bishop Berkeley, that

"Westward the course of Empire takes its way,"

were it a mere egotistic imagination, an ethnographical impertinence, to foresee that at no very remote time the descendants of those teeming bands of stout adventurous travellers who, a dozen centuries ago, in spite of Roman Emperors and Roman Legions, took possession of Europe, coming out of Asia, will take possession of Asia, coming out of America? Savages, they went out of Asia; they will enter it, men of the same force, armed with all the thousandfold might of science and invention. A race ahead of all other races in knowledge and mental power, and yet itself but partially unfolded, and in the full swing of eager progress, will meet on the populous shores of Eastern Asia, a people aged, stagnant, a completed people, a people that has long since run the range of its innate capacities, a people that has never travelled. The stronger a race is, the wider its travel.

What if we imagine the later waves of population, which, starting from the western slopes of the Himalayas, flooded, to fertilize, first Western Asia, then Eastern Europe, then Western Europe, then America, on their march displacing, or absorbing into their stronger blood less capacious breeds — what if we imagine them to have come full circle in their toilsome travel round the temperate zone of the globe, surging in triumphant splendor in the heart of ample Asia, brandishing, not the sword of war, but a far more potent instrument of conquest, the torch of Science, blazing with clear, accumulated, thoughtful might, illuminating domains at present undreamed of? What if we imagine this buoyant multitude, loaded with the mental spoils of thousands of years, starting again, to plant through Western Asia and Eastern Europe the benefactions of Science and Art and Culture, and the blessings that stream from the general usufruct of broad principles and intelligent submission to divine law, repeating, under far higher conditions, its westward travel, sowing everywhere, along its broadened furrow, truth and beauty and power?

XI.

OBEDIENCE.

Moving to the rhythm of law, the life that throbs from the mighty central soul gladdens with its pulse all the arteries of the Universe, forgetting never the finest capillaries of being. Of this animation the most sparkling result looks through the eyes of man. Within his wonderful self a man carries a triple life, each a boundless power, an unfathomable source, — his sensational or animal, what might be termed his fleshly life, his moral, spiritual, or passional life, which supplies the fuel and motive force to his being, and finally the life intellectual, whose office is that of the ship's rudder, to hold the combined lives to their natural or chosen courses. In this high function intellect is aided by instinct, which is a wise and innate, though unconscious, power of self-direction. But against the centrifugal forces within a man the two together, instinct and intellect, suffice not at times to keep his being in its natural orbit. The hardest to enlighten is selfishness.

Through the earlier phases of general human development, man delights in a youthful willfulness, a contradictory lawlessness, a partial self-destructive indulgence.

Among the later discoveries man makes is, that his well-being depends on obedience to law, and that the laws he is to obey are not usurping tyrannies, not even self-imposed restrictions, but movements of growth, impulses of healthy life, which invite kindly guidance in order to work as coöperative activities,— healthy vivacities, that only need sympathetic assistance and furtherance. Nature is as methodical and orderly as she is generous, and her generosity is only available to those who perceive and accept her method and her order.

What if you were to set yourself to quench the life of outward Nature, to arrest the rising grass in spring, to stay the cataract's leap, to cool the ripening rays of July: the very thought of such efforts savors of lunacy. Yet this is what every one now does daily, in greater or less degree. When, in eating or drinking, in overwork or underwork, asleep or awake, actively or passively, you break a law of Nature, you quench some of her life, and you quench it there where only it can be quenched, temporarily, partially, personally. You throw yourself out of the wardship of that beneficent wisdom which makes itself your sleepless, almost omnipotent, guardian and servant. And yet, such is the all-pervasive force of Nature, her inaccessible vitality, her irreducible might, and such our dependence upon her, our indissoluble ties to her, that with our worst lawlessness and willfulness we can but partially forfeit her protection. By resisting her demands, bodies, forms, are maimed or vitiated or destroyed, but the life that holds them in shape is inexpugnable. At the acme of willfulness, in the extreme darkness of desperation, a man commits suicide: his purpose is, to put an end to himself. He cannot do it: Nature's resource is too deep for his shallow strokes: she baffles him. The life that asserted itself by temporarily animating his organized body is inextinguishable, and keeps its hold for another phase of being. To his surprise, and at first to his dismay, he finds himself still alive: he has killed his body, his soul he cannot kill. Through his imperishable consciousness, he finds himself not only alive but retarded, obstructed by another, a crowning, breach of law.

XII.

FREEDOM.

THERE are who affirm, and try to believe, that indulgence of every impulse were enjoyment of freedom. When from present example and from history it is proved to them that such indulgence is ever followed by pain, penance, enslavement, death, then they exclaim that man has no freedom of will.

One-sided indulgence is license, not liberty. Is a man free to strike his neighbor because he is angry with him? Desire is not free will, it is not even will. To go whither impulse drives is to be the toy of desire or its victim. This is to be willful as children are. Every child, every man, has a will, many wills; but no children and few men, very few, have much freedom of will, which high condition is only then attained when there is coincidence between human and divine will, a condition only attainable through the full, harmonious activity of all of man's powers, and partially attainable through the habitual easy empire of the high moral powers over his wants and conduct. Only with completed human development can there be perfect freedom of will. A man's liberty is exactly in proportion to the degree of his unfolding. The chief men of Timbuctoo are immeasurably less free than the chief men of London. With human power in this broad sense human liberty ever grows.

The ancient destiny was the Greek conception of overruling law, checking, baffling, controlling human effort. But the Greek spiritual nature was not enough developed to conceive of this Divine law in its full beneficence and absolute justice. Hence the Greeks, and like them many moderns, nominal Christians, represent, and complain of, destiny as hard and cruel; which complaint is always an animal howl, or an egotistic agony.

Men in whom robust intellect, and strong animal or self-seeking passions are combined with what is called an iron will, have even less freedom of will than many who are intellectually and actively their inferiors. With the world such men often succeed in their aims; but if so, what they do is afterwards undone; for unfailingly as the physical law of light, the moral law asserts, sooner or later, its absolute, inevitable dominion. Force of will, thus combined, succeeds, at times largely, against men, never against God. Napoleon was the most godless man of his age. But mostly these bold, bad men, who never even near the condition of freemen, fail in their life-time, and die miserable and powerless, or gnaw their lives out on some St. Helena, or stalk about among their fellows under a ban, the harmless ghosts of their former selves, pointed at, but not heeded or heard.

To be unbound is no more to be free than to be strong in will and intellect is to be free. To be let loose is not only not to be enfranchised, it may be a step towards a wider disfranchisement. Within close tubes which carry their precious charge safe and unwasted to the minutest arterial ramifications, is confined the living blood. Make a breach in one of the tubes, and life flows away in the liberated current. A type is this of all being. Being, to be adequate, must be contained. The universe of being is a vast organic whole, one mighty combined unit made up of countless single units; and that the one whole abide in harmonious combination, and that each constituent enjoy its individual essential being, each must be withheld from infringing on its neighbors, must keep to its special path. Each is endowed with aptitudes, capacities, aspirations, the working of which constitutes its life. By misapplying these aptitudes, by balking these aspirations, it so far frustrates its life, and to that degree maims its freedom. When each is a law unto itself, it fulfills its end and feels itself free; that is, when by inward power and by integrity of aim, it completely obeys the law of its being, and thus fully unfolds its innate virtue. To violate this law is so much anarchy, a step back towards chaos.

To all life and movement law is a sheath of safety. And thence, man's best business is to study, discover, understand, and administer law. The laws which govern conscious human acts are moral laws, and as consciousness is the highest attribute of life, the laws which rule conduct are to man the most momentous. Equally with all other Divine laws they are inviolable. Every breach of them brings loss and an abridgment of freedom. Continuous breach of them leads to deeper and deeper servitude, ending in forfeiture of the privileges of consciousness, which forfeiture is moral death. What to the life of the body are the arterial tubes, which from the heart unrestingly carry blood to feed every corporeal function, such are the moral laws (issuing from his soul) which carry strength to the hourly conduct of the man. They confine and guide all its motions, that these, performing healthily their appointed offices, may enjoy their full life and freedom.

The organism of man is a hierarchy, wonderfully aggregated, beautifully proportioned, exquisitely adjusted out of seemingly oppugnant constituents. When all of these shall perform each its healthy function, will ensue active and most productive harmony. For the performance of its healthy function, not only does no one of these many and diverse constituents require the suppression or weakening of any other one, but not one of them, neither the highest nor the lowest in the scale, can reach its full function without the coöperation of each and all of the others. At the summit of the scale, the regulators of human movement are the generic feelings, the spiritual and moral sensibilities, whose approval is the touchstone of conduct, whose joy is the benediction of life, whose full satisfaction were the triumphant shout of freedom.

XIII.

THE BRAIN.

MEN have mind in proportion to brain. The brain of idiots weighs from fifteen to thirty ounces; the full, healthy human brain from forty to sixty. Mr. Davis of England, having a very large cranial collection, about eighteen hundred specimens from all quarters of the globe, ascertained the relative volume of brain of different races by filling the skulls with dry sand. He found that the European averaged 92 cubic inches, the Oceanic 89, the Asiatic 88, the African 86, the Australian 81. Measurements made by the late Dr. Morton of Philadelphia, who had a collection of over a thousand skulls, accorded in the main with those of Mr. Davis, and confirmed Blumenbach's scale of races, the Caucasian brain being the largest, the Mongolian the next in size, then the Malay, then the American Indian, the Ethiopian being the smallest.

The brain is made up of nerves and nervous substance; and in proportion as to the simplest form of brain (a mere rudimentary ganglion) parts are added, mental power increases. Not only is there no intellect and no emotion without nerves, there is no sensation, no voluntary movement. Nervous fibres enfold, embrace, penetrate into the body and its every limb and tissue: only through them can the whole and each part show life. Consider the power of nerves: they give to the swift his fleetness, to the strong his strength; without them no muscle can contract, no lung expand. These white threads are the conductors of force, the primary engines of motion, the arbiters of pain, the dispensers of joy. Now reflect, that of this most refined, most powerful material, this sublimated extract of matter, there are packed away in the scull from fifty to sixty ounces, from three to four pounds of a substance that has the highest potency among visible agents.

To think that for centuries naturalists, physiologists, philosophers, moralists, psychologists have had this tremendous battery of the soul darting at them messages which none of them could read. Before their eyes ever sparkled this divine treasury of revelations, and none learnt how to prize its transcendent worth; until, at the very end of the 18th century, a large-brained German, GALL, by one of those spontaneous springs of genius whereby the mind leaps from a fact to its law, got upon the track which after years of vigilant observation, patient, conscientious thought, led him to the discovery of the mighty function of this confluent, multitudinous, symmetric mass of nervous fibres, this conglomerate constellation of magnetic cells — led him to the discovery that this great organ of the mind (using *mind* to embrace all impulsive and emotional as well as intellectual movement) is not one single organ, but a congeries of organs, each the instrument of a separate mental power.

Pascal's saying that he could not conceive of a man without a head, has a deep significance when we reflect that Nature never makes two heads, any more than two faces or two leaves, alike, and that the differences in the size and shape of heads are caused and controlled by the mysterious irresistible motion of electrified nervous cords. To swap heads were to swap beings. The man is his head, or rather, that which shapes his head, the vivid inspired brain within it. Contrast the head of Napoleon with that of Murat, the head of Shakespeare with that of George III. the head of Pope Borgia with that of Melancthon. These contrasts hint at the creative potency of brain nerves. Run a line from just above the eyebrows backwards, an inch above the ear, and cut off the chin (which no mere animal has) and you have a type of the head and brain of animals next below man. The head, thus mutilated, is unhuman. To humanize it, instead of running the line horizontally from the root of the nose, run it vertically about three inches, and you have the outline of the forehead, the beaming forehead of man, "the front of Jove himself." But still, if from the top of this line you run another nearly at right angles to it with hardly any curve, you have not a man, you have a fearful creature with only animal propensities and intellect, an intellectual monster. But, from the top of the forehead spring an arch, and you have — in proportion to the height and width of the arch — a vaulting space for the play of those great cerebral organs, through whose instrumentality man has his high humanity, the organs of his broad generic feelings, his spiritual and moral powers.

Through the discoveries of Gall we are now enabled to make these impressive and most significant general partitions of the brain; but of such partitions Gall himself had at first no inkling. He started with no theory. The dawn of his discovery was in his schooldays, when, beaten in learning by rote by inferior classmates, he was led to observe, — urged doubtless by his vexation, — that those who excelled in verbal memory had mostly prominent eyes. To couple two such facts, at so early an age, denoted a scientific, philosophic capacity. Observing this coincidence at another school, and afterwards at the university, he conceived that the outward prominence was caused by the action of the brain. From this point the step was short to the conjecture, that if this were so there would be other similar conjunctions. Thus, year after year, he went on making observations and deductions from extremes of cranial conformation, visiting prisons, courtrooms, schools, hospitals, questioning friends and acquaintance, even accosting strangers in whom he perceived any remarkable configuration. In 1796, in his thirty-ninth year, he gave in Vienna, where he lived as a practicing physician, his first course of lectures on the physiology of the brain.

What is the fruit of Gall's work? This it is: (and when did the thought of man produce fruit of higher flavor and more nourishing?) that *the discovery of the function of the brain reveals the constitution of the human mind;* that the disclosure of the physiology of this huge, crowded, convoluted pile of precious, most expensive, nervous material opens wide at last the portal to the resplendent, immense, mysterious, unimaginably beautiful, temple of Psychology. Ponder the roll of mental faculties as here presented, presented in a distribution, before Gall not suspected or conceived of, which indeed could not have been imagined by any human intellect or combination of intellects, so proportioned is it, so logical, so penetrative, so divine. Not by intuition alone could this order and allotment have been seized or even approached, but only by the insight of genius, working patiently and lovingly upon the broadest, most various, most expressive, most pregnant of Nature's facts and phenomena.

Through the *objective* method what significant symmetry, what a philosophical evolution is here exhibited, which never could have been reached through the *subjective*. In intellectual movement what a graduated ascent from the individual to the generic ; from the powers that note the crowd of visible, tangible, physical objects, with their properties of form, size, weight, color, (properties common to all and inseparable from each) up through the relations of space and time and the infinitude of personal, historical, and scientific facts, to the great generalizing, combining faculties, the supreme intelligences, which enable men to provide, to organize, to forecast, to deduce, to classify, and which, engaged, in calm majestic action, to the service of the spiritual and moral sensibilities, with them unite to constitute the high Reason, that lordly, sacred gift, which empowers man, in the government of himself and his inheritance, the earth, to coact with the divine Regency.

By this objective process, observing and studying the brain intently, sagaciously, persistently, for years, Gall revealed likewise the wonderful organization and character of the other, and by much the larger division of the mind, the affective portion, that embracing the feelings. Here is displayed again a graduated ascension from the personal to the universal, from propensities to emotions, from the self-preservative to the self-expanding, from appetites and impulses, which man has in common with animals, to the wide, deep, disinterested sensibilities which make his humanity, from self-seeking dispositions up to innate senses of justice and reverence, to joy in the sublime and the beautiful, to faith, hope, and charity.

From the discoveries of Gall legitimate deductions are, that the brain is the instrument of mind; that the brain is not a single organ, but a congeries of organs, the function of each being to manifest a primitive mental power of feeling or of intellect; and that, other things being equal, such as health, temperament, opportunity, size is the measure of power.

Look now at the brain, or at the vaulted roof, which it builds for its protection, and shapes to its wants, that glittering crown to the upright majesty of man, that masterpiece of nature, which Gall's happy gift taught him to read with a vision so true as to discover its mighty function, through that discovery laying bare the structure and composition of the human mind, its power, aims, affiliations, which mental philosophers, from Plato to Hume, had been vainly trying to fathom with the ever short-coming help of their one dim method of self-consciousness. Note first the grouping of the mental organs. The perceptive, the elementary, intellectual, lie together along the base of the frontal brain. Similarly, the elementary affective, the organs of the domestic affections, the primary bonds among men, form another group at and near the base of the posterior brain. Then, between these two, along the sides and close together, are the energetic, pugnacious, and acquisitive feelings, what might be called the self-seeking propensities. Above this group, and above the domestic group, in the upper part of the rear of the head, come the organs of what may be termed the self-seeking sentiments. In front of these the feelings which give the glow of grandeur and of beauty to the whole mind, expanding it as by their position they expand the upper head laterally; and above these, in the coronal region of the brain, are the organs of the moral and spiritual sentiments, whose high office it is to control and temper all the other feelings, and which, when associated with the broad ratiocinative powers, — whose organs have the highest position in the forehead — present the noblest type of manhood.

Here then are presented the most important, the most significant facts that the boundless wealth of the immeasurable domains of nature can furnish, facts which offer to every man a clear picture, a clean analysis of his mental structure, the like of which for validity, distinctness, reality, was never even approached before, and which thus open the way to the solution of profoundest problems in psychical philosophy,—facts genuine, solid, not fancies honored as facts, facts purely objective, not "vain imaginations," as Bacon calls them, drawn out of a brooding brain, but transparent sunlit phenomena, brought to view by a discovery which, from the revelations involved in it, may be called sublime, and to which the dark delvings of the subtlest metaphysician are as the tentative accents of infancy to the resounding cadences of intelligent manhood from the mouth of authority.

The students and expounders of man's mental constitution, why have they not only failed to discern this sure source of light, but why, since it has been demonstrably exposed, do they so obstinately, so arrogantly despise it? Is this from spiritual and intellectual pride, from an egotistic repugnance to be beholden to aught but their own inward expedients, from that false independence which stiffens them into defiance of the supreme will, that self-sufficiency of human nature, typified in the revolt of Satan and the fable of the fall?

In some metaphysical organizations there is scientific ineptitude, causing tyranny of the subjective over the objective action; and thus, instead of steering their course by the blazing lights of Heaven, they grope tremulously, sounding forever in the fog of consciousness. Some philosophers never reach so high a plane of philosophy as to be beyond the shadows cast by the vulgar vice of jealousy. Some have not sympathy enough with life, with its infinite, and infinitely beautiful motions: they work in the rigid harness of the understanding, and so talk round and round a subject and never into it: their analysis is too meagre, too unfurnished, and so it never flowers into the bloom of synthesis. Some so much prefer turning on the axis of their own consciousness to turning their thought outward to the abundant glory and expressive glow of God's worlds, that for the beneficent unchanging laws of His founding they substitute shifting fancies and excogitated doctrines hardened into narrow postulates, into despotic dogmas, thus striving to make these, that is, conventional human ordinations, their rule of life, in place of the eternal injunctions of that transcendent supervisive power, the exploring of whose plans, the discovery of whose designs, is the best exercise of human intellect, the aspiring to know whose will is the most healthy movement of moral activities.

XIV.

MATERIALISM.

You have seen, observant reader, an old hen that has hatched a nest of ducklings; and did you mark her cackling astonishment and alarm, when for the first time she happens to bring her brood near a pond, and the little semi-aquatic fledglings, with a simultaneous joyful rush, all take to the water? Not from experience do they know that water is one of their elements. The materialists, and those who would make experience our sole teacher, are the puzzled hen, and set up a half angry cackle when you and I, spiritual earthlings, betake us to spirit as an element native to our nature, wherein we move with untaught delight, impelled, too, like the ducklings, by an innate impulse, and one infinitely higher and richer than that which drives them to the pond. If traceable antecedents were the sole causes, the cause of the ducklings taking to the water was the hen's happening to come near the pond. But what had her brood been chicks instead of ducklings?

A hundred bricks, set up in file, all go down one after the other. Is the fall of each of the hundred caused by the fall of each immediate antecedent, there being thus a hundred causes? Secondarily, it is; primarily, the fall of each and of the whole is caused by a mental movement, by a will directing a hand. So, every incident in our life is one of a series, acted on secondarily by an immediate antecedent, the primary source of the existence and condition of each incident being an intangible essence, a living power within us, superior to, predominant over, our outward acts.

To say that we learn everything from experience is to say that we get our all from circumstances, that is, from what is about us, which were to mistake influences for causes. Whence come circumstances? What are they? What can they be but pure creatures of mind, the busy product of past marriage between passion and intellect? All present existent circumstances must be the offspring of mind; they can have no other parentage, and their weight and multiplicity is in proportion to, is utterly dependent on, the force and quality of mental action. Were experience our only teacher, mankind would have remained uncivilized, for civilization can only be reached and advancement achieved through a series of thoughtful efforts, interior originalities, mental projections beyond experience. Of Columbus it may be said, that he first discovered the Western Continent in his brain, and then verified the discovery by experiment. The originator, the maker of facts, can be no other than mind, and mind controls the observation and employment of those already existing. Autonomic life the mind must have, or it could not be: some power of self-impulsion is implied in its being.

. The printed words that I am reading, whence are they? They come through the compositor's type-box. Where does he get them? In the manuscript before him. And the words in the manuscript, whence are they? From the mind of the writer. Every word is an offshoot from thought. Every deed of man is preceded by a thought. In the most trivial movement, immaterial action is the antecedent and producer of the material. Every result brought about by human contrivance and will is an embodied finishing whose beginning is a spiritual seed sown in the brain. No grossest act but existed first in thought before it took body. Without thinking, a man would go without his dinner. Every act proves a precedent thought. This is an absolute law of mind. As all human acts presuppose human thought, so superhuman acts presuppose superhuman thought. A man is a superhuman act, and the existence of a man demonstrates the preëxistence of God. But materialists not being willing to entertain the idea of God, this exposition will not be accepted by minds in which, to use the language of Mr. Hazard in his profound work[1] on "Causation and Freedom in Willing," "admiration of the minutely perfect is much more active than admiration for the sublimely vast," minds not endowed to enjoy, and therefore to profit by, thoughts on the infinite and immeasurable, minds not open to mysterious suggestions.

Most men, even among the highly organized, are defective in one direction or other. Some are born without, or with very weak, musical sensibility; some with small faculty of reasoning; others without feeling for the beautiful; Dr. Johnson had no sense of smell. Material-

---

[1] Two Letters on *Causation and Freedom in Willing*, addressed to John Stuart Mill. By Rowland G. Hazard. Boston: Lee & Shepard, 1869.

ists are born with feeble spiritual intuition. They are truncated, and truncated at the top. They lack the higher imagination; they know not the sublimity of awe. Their spiritual senses are dull. Hence their minds are comparatively superficial, and are insufficient.

Metaphysics, having to do with the laws of mind and of being, *must* deal with the spiritual. Nay, spiritual intuitions, emotional susceptibilities, are the best of its substance. The man who cannot turn a tune, who takes no delight in Beethoven or Bellini, would you go to him for the laws and capacities of music? Strictly speaking, a materialist cannot be a metaphysician, a mental philosopher. His cannot be what æsthetically is called a creative mind; and to be a good mental philosopher, there must be a power of intuitive perception that is akin to the creative gift of high poetry. Tell him, with Epictetus, that he is a soul bearing about a corpse, and he will deem your talk foolishness. And yet, to get thoroughly at any movement, or even at any condition of being, there is but one track, and that is along the line of light that flashes from our own soul into the soul of things. By no other can the intellect penetrate beyond surfaces. "The only cause," I quote again from Mr. Hazard, "of which we have any idea, is the exercise of sufficient power in the effort of an intelligent being."

Was the fall of an apple the *cause* of the discovery of gravitation, or only the occasion? Was not the cause in the mental aptitude of Newton for taking a hint from nature, and for tracing ordinary superficial phenomena to their deep source? On that same day hundreds of eyes saw apples fall, but only the brain of Newton so seized the spectacle as to see it with interior vision; he got behind the phenomenon. And still behind this Newtonian cause of the discovery of gravitation, was there not that supreme cause which endowed him to make the discovery? In living phenomena and motion to see only a quality of matter, is to merge spirit in matter, to dethrone mind, and subordinate it to things. By the habit of doing this we grow short-sighted, defrauding ourselves, unmanning ourselves, by a voluntary circumscription, a psychical semi-suicide.

XV.

THE LIFE TO COME.

[The following was written to a friend in the country, a scholar and thinker, a refined thoughtful writer, who alternates studious in-door work with agricultural enjoyments, and the improvement of helpful animal breeds. In the letter, to which this is an answer, this gentleman had thrown out distrusts and paradoxical hints, to pique and prompt his correspondent.]

WHEN, to provide winter food for your cattle, you plant turnips, you look sharply to the seed; and when they are sprouted you do your best to have them grow thriftily from week to week, from month to month, so that may be most fully attained their end as healthful bovine nutriment. You overlook their whole life, and at the very first stage your thought runs to the last, each successive stage being a step in a progression. The same with your sheep. You strive for the best breeds to begin with, that the final outcome of wool or mutton may be satisfying. Every day of each individual animal is a preparation for the following day, an advancement upon the preceding.

For your little boy this provident looking ahead is still more eager, and far more comprehensive; and while you are ever watchful that each day shall be a solid basis for to-morrow, your imaginations are leaping forward to his school-days, his college-days, his manhood, his wedding-day, his ripeness and success. The present is father to the future, is ever shaping it. By a logical bond, indissoluble, the two are bound together; and the higher, the more life-saturated, the more significant and prophetic the being of the creature is, the more pregnant is the bond, and the more precious each link in its inseparable enchainment. Your life is a palpitating, categorical continuity (that has an Alemannic smack that you will like), each consecutive joint of it a transmitter of the past to the future, its earlier throbs as necessarily linked to the later as are the flashes of the two termini of a telegraphic cable. The end cannot be sundered from the beginning. And when and where is the end?

In your interesting, suggestive letter of March 10, you say: "I would willingly leave unsolved all the questions of the life to come, if any teacher would tell me how to settle those of this life." But is not to-morrow, next month, next year, a part of our life to come? The man who is indifferent to what is to happen to him next week or next year is likely to find himself, by and by, in the poor-house; for if he neglects to look providently toward his life to come, this will be done for him; it *must* be done by somebody. A turnip's life reaches its end in six months, a sheep's in as many years, and a man's its earthly end in as many decades. They who guard his childhood, if they are good guardians, have ever in mind his future stages, his life to come. " In bringing up a child, think of its old age," says deep Joubert. Is a man's life like a turnip's or a sheep's, to end here " on this shoal of time," in dust? Is a man but a brain-crowned *corpus*, temporarily endued with volition and ratiocination and imagination and aspiration? After getting rid of this body, I should not like to find myself in the poor-house of spirits.

"What has religion to do with Heaven?" you ask. Religion is the wakefulness of those sensibilities which bind our present being to its future trans-earthly being, involving thus a consciousness and acknowledgment of, and a submission to, the vast invisible creative might that encompasses us. Sensation, caution, and intellect combine to watch providently over our bodies; religion performs a like office for our souls. As sensation warns us against what is hurtful to body, spiritual sensibility warns us what is hurtful to soul, especially in the life which is to come after the fleshly envelope shall have been cast. The being of the body implies shape and size; the being of the soul implies religious appetence. If we have souls, or, to speak more philosophically, if we are souls, we must be religious; that is, we must feel ourselves coupled to the Infinite Soul, must be liable to be prompted to aspire toward the Eternal, be ever capable of feeling that we are in a sublime, unimaginably resplendent presence, be subject to moods of admiration and awe at thought of the invisible Mightiness. Men are spirits. Their being spirits gives them this transcendent privilege. Had they it not, they were not spirits, and might adopt as their creed the saying of one of the sprightly interlocutors in Beaumarchais' famous comedy, the "Mariage de Figaro:" —

"Boire quand on n'a pas soif, faire l'amour en touts temps — il n'y a que ça qui nous distingue des autres bêtes."

Wordsworth's wish, which he applied to his life on earth, —

> "And I could wish my days to be
> Bound each to each by natural piety,"

should embrace our whole life, so that from the earth-stage we may pass without jar or fall or disappointment to the ultra-earth stage.

> "They end not here, our appetites —
> On earth they but begin:
> For though our bodies rot, their rights
> Survive as bliss or sin.
>
> "A marriage deep, without divorce,
> Is that of spirit and flesh,
> And from the cold relapsing corpse
> Springs life forever fresh.
>
> "The body's members are no toys
> For the soul's sublunar play:
> But counters that, in griefs or joys,
> Sum what the soul must pay.
>
> "How fruitful is the littleness
> Wherewith our souls are vext,
> When acorns of this world express
> Oaks rooted in the next."

You refer to the vexed and vexing problem of the existence of evil. Could we get a view of our world from a high enough point, might we not possibly discover that there is nothing absolutely evil? By aid of the microscope our physical vision finds beauty in mouldiest clods, wonders in dullest matter. Were our moral vision similarly armed, might not that look globular and symmetrical which now seems flat and deformed, that useful which now seems obstructive, that attractive which is now repulsive, that beneficent which now looks malignant? In the bounded view we commonly get we often find that what we thought a calamity proves a benefaction. What we call evil is *always* a consequence of a breach of law. To tell your son that his toothache is caused by the breaking of a physiological law by him, or his parents, or his grandparents, will not, to be sure, check the pain; nor do I think the toothache a spiritual lever. But man can learn — and it is the most fruitful of his lessons — that law is absolute, and in its aim beneficent; that aim being, along with growth, stability, conservation, improvement. Whichever way we turn we are met by law, and we soon perceive that law is uniform and irresistible, and that we prosper in proportion as we conform ourselves to its behests. Could we always submit us to law, physically, morally, intellectually, spiritually, we should be completely prosperous. Law is an ever-active ideal, above us, around us, correcting us, guiding us, cultivating us, inviting us, exalting us. The nations and the individuals that have discovered and that obey the most and deepest laws are the most advanced and the wisest and best.

But why are not all laws laid bare in a way that we could follow and obey them all, and thus escape suffering? This would be making the earth a Methodist heaven. How would you like to do nought but sing hallelujahs for seventy years? Let us all be made perfect, and we should have no goal beyond us, no summit above us to climb at, no motive to movement, and thence no joy in mental life, whose great spring and privilege is activity, aim, projection, progress, and whose greatest delight is to grasp something out of the unknown and add it to the known. To be aye reaching up for a higher, to be open forever to new revelations, to grow unceasingly — such is the birthright of man. What a destiny! how vast, how beautiful! What various and boundless range of life! Mere animals have only a sensuous, sensual range, and that momentary and short. Your favorite ram can only see from one field to another; you can behold stars that are so far off their light has been thousands of years in coming to your eye; and in thought you can travel beyond the visible spheres, and you can think of and believe in a happy endless hereafter. That men can so believe is the subtlest proof of their spirituality and immortality. In a sound mind is there an anticipation that cannot be fulfilled?

Don't distress yourself because "the big fish eat the little fish, and the little fish eat mud." Their mode of life and of death is accommodated to their sensibilities. Mud is as grateful to the palate of the fish that eats it as woodcock is to yours; and woodcock is after all but a cunning elaboration of mud. But why so much death? Why this terrible catastrophe? Wherefore die at all? Because without daily removal by death the surface of the earth would grow encumbered with matter, and thus would get to be a moving dung-heap. Besides, death being "most in apprehension," animals escape the worst of it; and as it is seen that men who have suffered from this apprehension meet death calmly and without fear, we may infer that it is made easy to animals. And to men it has been made fearful chiefly by shallow, spurious, extravagant, *infernal* (don't miss the pun) theologies. Death is not a catastrophe; it is not a coming to an end. It is a crisis of change, a bridge of transition into another state. In the case of animals, it is logical transformation; in the case of man, it is logical promotion.

The creative Mightiness and sufficiency manifest themselves in *Law*. Law is perfection. It is no sign of "deficiency of power" in the creative mind that we and all about us are created imperfect. Imperfection is demanded for what constitutes the life of life, progression, the joy of change, the delight of improvement, the exhilaration of ascent. Law, being perfect, is ever beckoning us toward perfection. Human life could not be lived without hope; and hope implies a something brighter and better and happier in the future, and implies therefore a present imperfection and a growth out of it. Imperfection is the ground whence spring up stimulants to motion, to activity, to aspiration. Without imperfection there were no expectation, no curiosity, no color, no ecstasy, on earth neither smiles nor tears, neither comedy nor tragedy.

> "Life, like a dome of many-colored glass,
> Stains the white radiance of Eternity."

Were life pure white, it would be monotonous, tedious, lifeless, beside being invisible.

Toward the end of your letter you say, "Cannot you write me a few lines, comforting and instructive?" When you wrote these words you violated a law — that of prudence; and so you are visited with the evil of these many pages. Look out, when you walk among rattlesnakes, not to break this law again, but provide yourself against "the serpent's tooth" with thick leggins; for the serpent has as much right to his venom as man has to his, and ejects it less malignantly.

XVI.

BOOKS FOR BOYS.

(IN A LETTER TO A LADY.)

To the bounded extent that it can be granted, willingly I grant the request of your earnest letter. "How shall I educate my son that he may become a wise and happy man?" this is what you ask. Could any one, could a convocation of the wisest, be sure of teaching you this? A child is too vivid an individuality, that its coming character be so absolutely moulded from without. Nevertheless, for children much may always be done, in most cases very much, and especially where there is will and intellect moved by a love so deep as yours for your boy. "Tell me what books are best for him: there are so many books." Many, and yet so few that will nourish the mind of a child or a youth. You, perhaps, think that to one versed in books an answer to this question will be easy. Were you to ask me how most naturally, and therefore healthfully, to feed your son's body, I should say, — give him bread (*good* bread) and fruit and water. Let no *flattering* food touch his palate, and above all, no stimulant in meat or drink. As to what should be set before his mind, follow the same principle. Keep away from him all pages in which there is thought or feeling exaggerated, or forced, or insidiously attractive; in which there is anything one-sided, or superficial, or delusive — in a word, all pages in which there is falsehood however dressed or disguised. Let him not be cheated by what he reads. The food of his mind should be clean and sweet with sincerity and truth — truth of fact, truth of principle, truth of feeling.

But this you know: you wish to be told the names of the books whose pages will be wholesome for your boy. Were he six or eight years older, I could more readily tell you. I have known, however, of young readers, not over twelve years, who, of their own motion, took to Shakespeare. If your son has not done so, try him with "The Tempest," or "Twelfth Night," or "As You Like It," or "Much Ado About Nothing." Shakespeare is the best reading I know for minor or adult. There is in Shakespeare more fidelity and fullness, more sense and purity, more liveliness and solidity, more truth and more poetry, than in any other writer. His large faculty of wonder stretches open the minds of the young, which are then filled with images of beauty. They can take in but a part of him, but their imaginations are warmed and grandly peopled. Intellect and feeling are both educated by his pages as they will be by no others. If a boy can gain admittance to the personages of Shakespeare, they are the best company he can keep. When with them, a child of intelligence and sensibility will be fascinated, he knows not why, Shakespeare is so full of blood, so full of soul.

Good biographies, well-told lives of the truly great, are excellent reading for the young. We have two that American boys should delight in — Washington and Columbus, by Irving. Here, while storing his brain with the doings and personality of two supreme men, the young reader has the gain of unconsciously learning history. Franklin's autobiography is not a book for the very young. Plutarch is always a resource ; I wish we had a livelier, more idiomatic English version. A dozen years ago an admirable life of the Chevalier Bayard was published in New-York, written by W. Gilmore Simms. There are, I believe, several Lives of

Sir Philip Sidney. These two rose to so rare a moral height, that their characters and conduct are inspiring models. John Forster, of the Inner Temple, is the author of valuable "Lives of Eminent British Statesmen," leaders in the Great Rebellion, Pym, Hampden, Cromwell, Vane, Marten. So closely are their careers interwoven with national events, these events themselves being the wrestling of great principles, that the report of the parts played by these eminent actors is more reflective than narrative. But the period and the conflict are so stirring and momentous, that an aspiring tractable boy will not be therefore repelled. Besides, boys, when once mounted on the narration, have a ready way of galloping across the reflective field

Hartley Coleridge wrote three volumes about "Northern Worthies," Andrew Marvell, Bentley, Lord Fairfax, Lady Anne Clifford, Roger Ascham, Captain Cook and others — an instructive series, scholarly, conscientious, sound in feeling and written in good English. Hartley had much of the fine quality of his great father, S. T. Coleridge. Wrangham's "British Plutarch," in six volumes, has some value, containing brief biographies of one hundred noted

Englishmen, from Wolsey to Nelson. But it wants both research and style. The latter want would make it distasteful to boys, for these have a quick feeling for life and light in the printed page.

History — which is the biography of nations — dealing with organic masses, is but partially within reach of immature intelligence, and of histories written for the young one should be mistrustful. That they be well executed, artistic as well as historic gifts are needed. Even then, in trying to adapt the account of complicated events and characters to the simplicity of the youthful mind, there is danger that both be falsified. Thus to qualify history, without unmanning it, is next to impossible. Could not a capable boy of 12 or 14, who likes to read, fasten himself upon Motley's "Rise of the Dutch Republic," and its continuation, "The History of the United Netherlands"? Here, told with the animation of sympathy, is the story of a handful of heroic men who, through two generations, carried on, with unsurpassed courage, persistency and self-sacrifice, against the then most powerful empire on the globe, a struggle for the dearest rights of manhood, ending in a success which was a gain to the whole of Christendom. In following the fortunes of the indomitable Hollanders, the reader hugs to his heart their sublime leader, and a boy can have no intimates more profitable, more precious, than William the Silent and Washington; but he must have it in him to make them his friends by loving and admiring them.

For a boy's reading tne difficulty is to get books with a soul in them — books that one can shake hands with, so real are they and so attaching. The same with his teachers — one teacher will make attractive what under another will be repulsive. As to what studies (beyond the universally necessary for every educated man) will be most suitable for your son, that will depend on his individual proclivities; whether his talents be literary or scientific or artistic; whether he be inwardly impelled to action or to quiet studiousness. Men of action are mostly not given to books; and boys, whose bent is decidedly toward action, will not be furthered by an enforced attention to reading and study. Nor are artists apt to be fond of the printed page; their business is to express, to give out, not to absorb from others. The three or four most distinguished artists I know read little. In the school-books of boys, who have plastic gifts, the pages most used will be the blank fly-leaves, which will be found covered with drawings and figures. If your son has a well-defined tendency, a proved inclination for any particular field of work or study, encourage him in that. What a boy goes at with love he will do well. The choice of nature should always be accepted.

But the moral side — thence it is that come your deepest anxieties. The hopes that are the joy of a natural mother are daily darkened by thoughts of the dangerous world your child is soon to enter and work in. To the maternal imagination he is on the border of an ominous wilderness, where crouch wolves and serpents ready to howl and hiss — where reigns a lurid twilight terrible with baited traps and masked pitfalls. For your son you "dread youth and young manhood." You have suffered yourself, you see others suffer from the malice, or falsehood, or coldness, or rapacity of those around them. But within you was an *inner energy* before which evil slank away and danger quailed. A triumphant mother, you have brought your child through twelve years which you almost shudder to look back upon. Has not he a manful share of this inward power for self-protection? Has he not that in him through which you can make him feel so intense a *self-respect*, that he shall be able to walk through temptation and corruption unstained and unbowed? It is a something higher than pride, stronger than self-reliance, this feeling of thorough self-respect. It is a soul-energy, which masters the whole being for its good, which watches with a vigilance to which even that of dutiful mothers is drowsiness. It is the sense of duty and the sense of honor held in hand by the divine individuality within. Make your son keenly aware of this pure lofty self, with its tutelary authority. Make him conscious that always, everywhere, in all cases, in every emergency, trial, solicitation, he carries within him an inseparable angel, to warn, shield, and rescue him; make him really know this, and you may loosen "your mother's arms around him." He hears a voice surer, more awakening, more commanding, aye, even more purifying than a "mother's whispers." You would like him to have friends; these are good for him to have. You would like to be ever so near him, as to be yourself his never-failing friend; this were good. But all this is naught to making himself his friend. All men may be helped by friends; we all can and should help one another; but finally, no one can save a man but himself; and he or she who makes him fully aware of this is his best friend outside of himself. Out of your own strong warm heart teach your son to value himself; not from pride or ambition or through self-comparison with others, but through a clear overpowering sense of personal responsibility, responsibility to his higher self; teach him this, and you "put upon him plate-armor which shall shield him," not from all suffering and sorrow on this temporary earth, where our chief business should be to better ourselves spiritually — there are sorrows and sufferings that are purifying and invigorating — but from harm from without. Thus will be averted or neutralized the hostile influences that still ply around a young man, ever ready to assail him. You do a high duty in getting the best teachers you can for your son, in teaching him yourself; but his best teacher is himself. All his life, should he live to a hundred, should be education, and the best of it self-education. But I must close. What I have here set down, although so fragmentary and insufficient, makes a long letter; if you get from it a hint or two, or a corroborating breath of sympathy, it will not have been written in vain.

XVII.

FREDERICK WILLIAM ROBERTSON.

I WOULD pay my share of tribute to the character, qualities, and doings of a man who in the past few years has become dear to very many far beyond the precincts of his parish in Brighton, England, where, in 1853, he died at the early age of thirty-seven.

Men there are with such fullness of the higher life in their brains that they overflow procreatively upon their fellows. Of this chosen few was Robertson, one of those deep, pure, abundant human springs that, at far intervals along our track, gush up strong and clear, where all may drink and be slaked, the laborer and the lord, the scholar and the artisan, man and woman. The depth and beauty and limpidity and, I will add, the practicality, of Robertson's teaching all come from its spirituality. Few are as intelligent as he; and so spiritually-minded I know, in our generation, of no man who has been in the public eye. He was a many-sided man, morally and intellectually. Had he not been what he became, — a light such as shone from no other pulpit within the British realm, — he might have made himself an influential parliamentary orator, or a far-eyed military leader, foremost in the advance, or a brilliant scientific expounder. Into a close tissue were woven threads various, rich, elastic, to give strength and beauty to the vocation which his father, with a wise instinct, chose for him.

The ruling principle of Robertson's life was dutifulness. At the command of this he sacrificed his preference for the army to submit him to the preference of his father. Having done so, he threw the whole of his rare energies into the work of qualification. One of the first of his self-imposed tasks was, to imbue himself with the New Testament; and this task he set about with so earnest a will that in a short time he had the whole by heart, the Greek as well as the English. The qualities requisite to make a clergyman what he should be, he enumerates in the ninth lecture on St. Paul's Epistle to the Corinthians: "Great powers of sympathy; a mind masculine in its strength, feminine in its tenderness; humbleness; wisdom to direct; that knowledge of the world which the Bible calls the wisdom of the serpent; and that knowledge of evil which comes rather from repulsion from it than from personal contact with it." A conscientious man, with this ideal of his life-work, would not have easy years. To such a one the cardinal question, *what is truth?* would press urgently. Ceaselessly disturbed by discontent with himself, Robertson at times would exclaim, "I am nothing but a stump-orator." Seeing the crowds that choked his church, Sunday after Sunday, and the breathless attention he constrained them to, he would, in moments of over-anxious self-examination, reproach himself with drawing and holding this throng through the mere gifts of the platform-speaker; whereas into these discourses he so poured his life, past and present, that, as one of his intimate friends, Lady Byron, said of him, "he was *sowing* himself beyond his strength." In the pulpit he spoke out, as in his daily doings he strove to act out, what at the close of the great sermon on "Caiaphas' view of Christian Sacrifice" he lays down as the true human life: "Life is elevation of soul — nobleness — divine character. The spirit of Caiaphas was death: to receive all and give nothing;

to sacrifice others to himself. The spirit of Christ was life: to give and not receive; to be sacrificed, and not to sacrifice. Hear Him again — *He that loseth his life, the same shall find it.* That is life: the spirit of losing all for Love's sake. That is the soul's life, which alone is blessedness and heaven." Ever is this one of his inspiring themes. In the beautiful discourse in the same volume (the first) on the *new commandment of Love to one another*, he thus comments on the mocking speech, *He saved others, himself he cannot save:* " Unconsciously these enemies were enunciating the very principle of Christianity, the grand law of all existence, that only by losing self can you save others; that only by giving life you can bless."

One of Robertson's friends said, " His life is in his sermons." That the sermons were the fruit of his life, of his inmost movement, that in them he exhibited what he was and what he strove to be, — to this was due their sustained thrilling power over his weekly hearers, and to this too, is due that we, his readers, are by them so warmed, so uplifted. Nowhere is there a trace of sentimentality, of feeling assumed or super-subtleized or thinly expanded;

nowhere any ostentation of intellectuality, of dialectic gymnastics. He is always cordial, always in earnest. His sermons are aglow with a large lucent soul: they pulsate with spiritual life: they are mellow with the finest juice of humanity. Thence are they so deeply, so uniquely attractive. The life written in these great discourses is the literary oratorical embodiment of the searchings and the meditations, the bafflings and the aspirations, of his daily, hourly, unwritten life, — the projection of his luminous personality into public prominence. In Robertson there was no vicious dualism: he never seemed what he was not. His preaching had its roots in his individual strivings after a better practice; and when his words grow gorgeous and tremulous in delineating possible blessedness, they rise on the wings of a healthful imagination, not on the bubbles of a wordy redundance.

A mind so progressive, eager, susceptible, would be especially sensitive to the winds of doctrine which, at the period of Robertson's entrance into the Church, were blowing in strong counter-currents over the sea of English theology. The *Tractarians* were in the full momentum of their retrogressive movement.

For a while he rolled somewhat unsteadily amid the conflicting waves of controversy, and it was only after his settlement in Brighton, that he became so clear and firm in his convictions as to sail right onward with confidence and steady self-reliance. Of the five volumes of sermons, — all preached at Brighton in the last six years of his life, — the chief burthen is, CHRISTIANITY IS A LIFE, NOT A CREED. His "Master" was his ever present exemplar; and nowhere is the spirituality of that sublime lonely life set forth more vividly.

"To saturate life with God, and the world with Heaven, that is the genius of Christianity." "God is the father of the whole human race, and not of a mere section of it: a divine spirit is the source of all goodness in man: the righteousness acceptable in his sight is not ceremonial, but moral, goodness: the only principle which reconciles the soul to God, making it one with God, is self-sacrifice: this is the essence of Christianity." "The first lesson of Christianity is this, — Be true; and the second this, — Be true; and the third this, — Be true." "Christ's rule was, if any man will *do* his will. A blessed rule, a plain and simple. Whatever else may be wrong, it must be right to be pure, to be just and tender, and merciful and honest. It must be right to love, and to deny one's self. Let him *do* the will and he shall know. Observe; men begin the other way. They say, if I could but believe, then I would make my life true. If I could but be sure what is truth, then I would set to work to live in earnest. No; God says, Act — make the life true, and then you will be able to believe: Live in earnest, and you will know the answer to what is truth." "The Pharisees could conceive no goodness free, but only that which is produced by rewards and punishments, — law goodness, law righteousness : to dread God, not to love and trust Him, was their conception of religion. And this, indeed, is the ordinary conception of religion." Expansions of these and similar central sentiments are, for the most part, the substance of Robertson's discourses. Mysteries he makes transparent by the solvent of common sense, — common sense, as so happily defined by the Duke of Wellington in a conversation with Rogers, — "a good understanding modulated by a good heart." The heart of Robertson was a deep spring of sympathies, wrought by a strong compact intellect into showers, through which there sparkled so divine a light that it entranced, while warming and refreshing, the hearts of his hearers. And his style partakes of the power and beauty of this union. It has that throbbing vivacity, that elastic undulation, which style may have when thought has been steeped in the riches of a soul.

Never did man more faithfully follow his own great primary precept — Be true. He was true to all his duties, true to his fellow men in every relation, true to himself. Manliness, in the heartiest meaning of the word, he had. To him may be applied what Napoleon said after his interview with Goethe, — "There you have *a man*." The blessing he was to so many near and around him has not ceased with his life on earth: we feel it through the record left of his speech and his deeds. The glowing words he uses to describe St. Paul might serve for his own epitaph: "A heart, a brain, and a soul of fire: all his life a suppressed volcano: his acts, 'living things with hands and feet:' his words, 'half battles.'"

XVIII.

GOETHE'S FAUST.

The poet must make himself *one* with his subject, which then comes from him new-born, steeped in the juice of his own being. This he can only do through intense sympathy; and thence, to reproduce a large deep subject (a tragedy of Hamlet or of Lear) the poet must have a large deep nature. His heart must throb with the heart of what he would create, else he can not create it. Into Faust, as his masterpiece and the longest of his poetic works, Goethe put more of himself than into any other. The principles he had thought out; the knowledge he had ripened; the temptations, joys, trials, vexations, he had undergone, his aspirations and his disappointments — all is in Faust; the depths of his mind, the woes of his heart — all transfigured by poetry. Never did poet, saving Dante, put so much of himself into a single poem, nor was there ever poet, saving Shakespeare, who had so much to put in.

When Coleridge said that the Faust of

Goethe wants causation, he said what is true; but when he meant this as a reproach, it seems to me he was mistaken. Faust is not, and is not called, a drama. The title-page reads, "Faust, a Tragedy." It is a lyrical tragedy. Goethe's organization was lyrical, not dramatic. His æsthetic forte was the utterance of feeling in song, ballad, elegy, narrative, or dialogue; and when, in order to have scope for characterization, in which he was a master, he chose dialogue, the production was dramatic in form, more than in essence. It would have no dramatic shock of incidents, no rapid material progression, no stirring muscular movement, no shifting interaction of hostile personages, but would give embodiment to an interplay of strong or tender emotion, to inward struggles, to overflow of passionate feeling, wrought into scenes vivid and varied and stamped with beauty of form. Such are "Iphigenia" and "Tasso," and even "Egmont" — all dramas in outward shape, — lyric expansions in dialogue.

Goethe was warned against Faust as a subject that has already been often treated, and with small results. Wise monitors! As if to a poet the subject were anything more than a mould, and a pliable, expansible mould, into which to pour himself. His predecessors had failed, because they had little or nothing to put into the mould. Faust, as being a popular legend, and a popular legend sprung out of the depths of the human soul, lent itself with ease to genuinely poetic treatment, and especially to a poet of such manifold endowment as Goethe, whose lyrical predilections, too, had here, in the legendary character of the theme, a clear field for indulgence. There was no need to bind the scenes in dramatic continuity, in logical necessity: they could be kept close enough together by the flowing reins of emotional control, held in hand by the boldest artistic invention. From its compass and free privileges, the subject was particularly attractive to Goethe, who clung to it all his life, taking it up in early manhood and completing it in his eighty-second year.

Goethe had such facility of expression that he was only saved from running into verbiage by his strong and exacting intellect, and he had such fullness of sensibility that he was only saved from sentimentalism by his sound ethic as well as æsthetic feeling. But this rare combination and balance of high qualities give a precision and compactness to his expression, and a closeness to the texture of his thought, which make him in his best pages — and his best pages count by thousands — an author difficult to translate; and, of all his poems, Faust is the most difficult. And yet Faust must be translated. The light therein must not be hidden away from all the rest of the reading world under the wrappage of a single language. And we can say, without being chargeable with American brag, that the two best translations of Faust into English have been made by two of our countrymen, Mr. C. T. Brooks, and Mr. Bayard Taylor.

Christianity, civilization, progress, have been, and are now more than ever, nourished by translations. What if Isaiah and Job and David do lose somewhat of their original poetic sheen in the transit from Hebrew into English. Without translation we should have had no Bible — not a chapter. What do we of this remote generation not owe to the translators of Plato and Plutarch? As the nations of Christendom grow more and more united, the more is the need, the greater the service, of translation for the furtherance of science, literature, advancement, freedom. Goethe is one of the master minds of the world. His sixty volumes are in themselves a literature; his pages are full of wisdom and light; and, of all his beautiful creations, Faust is the most original and the most commanding.

Goethe declares that "he who cannot get it into his head that *spirit* and *matter*, *soul* and *body*, *thought* and *extension*, or, as a late French writer expresses it, *will* and *movement*, were, are, and ever will be the necessary double ingredients of the Universe, which demand for themselves equal rights, and therefore both together may be looked upon as representatives of God — that man should give up all attempt to be a thinker, and give all his days to the common noisy business of the world." Goethe's spirituality admitted matter to an equal alliance: he would not therefore have given assent to Joubert's position: "To create the world a grain of matter sufficed; for all that we see, this mass which affrights us, is nothing but a grain which the Eternal has created and set to work."

In the second part of Faust there might be, along with the purification through outward activity, an inly-originating and inly-working emotion, tending to cleanse and uplift the whole man and his doings, giving to his activities larger scope and deeper meaning. This inward self-stirred spiritual source was not so deep in Goethe as to play in his greatest creation a controlling part. Faust sweeps through a wide circle, but here was a segment of it which he passed over, without getting from it all the light it is capable of imparting.

The product of a nature so rich, thoughtful, and true, Faust involves sound moral lessons. Through the depth and wisdom of his writings Goethe has done much to condemn and correct the very aberrations himself fell into. As poet-thinker, he did more than any man of his age to clear the general atmosphere.

XIX.

SHELLEY.

IF to have the power to lift his theme into a light so fresh, so penetrating, that it reveals sides, qualities, relations, never presented before, — a light self-kindled in the lifter's soul; if to be full of thoughts, images, conceptions, as new as beautiful, and so full of them that they are irresistibly urgent for rhythmical utterance, and when uttered give a new delight and a new virtue to the capable reader; if to exalt the earthly that it shall look heavenly, to irradiate the common that it shall glisten with unsuspected life, to make the motions of daily being converge to a focus so lastingly brilliant that men's eyes are drawn to it through the ages, their vision being thereby purged and strengthened; if to be and do all this is to be a poet, Shelley takes rank among the foremost of those whose function it is to enkindle and refine and elevate and liberate their fellow-men. Rays shot from a central core, ever aflame with love and aspiration, are the lines of Shelley. Than his poems more genuine emanations from a poet's inmost were never penned. Through them throbs a great heart, the heart of an earnest, unselfish, loving man; and this manly throb gives substance and an added brilliancy to their poetic sparkle.

In literature to create is to breathe a soul into your theme. Divest "Hamlet" of Shakespeare, and it is a vulgar tale of lusts clotted with blood. Take the poetry out of "Midsummer Night's Dream," and Theseus and Hypollita and Hermia and their fellows are graceless egotists, whose talk one would not tolerate for five minutes; and Oberon and Titania and Puck, those everlasting most vivacious of realities, would suddenly sink out of sight into the earth, as being now more valueless than the weeds which deform its surface, for these have roots and a life in them. Ask the first man you meet what he has to say of the West Wind. The liveliest answer you would get would be one like that of the lady who, when her companion uttered his delight at the frisking play of lambs in a field, said, she preferred them with mint sauce. A clever man and a ready might, without shame, have naught to say of the West Wind. Now read Shelley's ode, to learn what a marvelously poetical theme it may be made by a great poet who puts himself into it in one of his best moods.

The "Ode to the West Wind" is especially characteristic of Shelley, because it is so purely poetical; for when Shelley is most himself, his mind is most creative, he being essentially, predominantly, a poet. And the poet is most a poet when he can spin a lasting web out of his own brain. This Ode is furthermore characteristic of Shelley because it is so self-evolved, thought awakening thought interminably within him, imagination then wafting him from peak to peak of multitudinous sunlit creation. This rapid procreative energy is a mark of the highest mental resource, involving intellectual originality with swift and wide imaginative swing. Note, in the following passage, how image shoots out of image, impromptu fertility lavishing poetic wealth, and with a logical fitness that keeps the shifting stream firmly bordered. Every comma is a momentary pause before a new bound.

"O thou
Who chariotest to their dark wintry bed
The wingéd seeds, where they lie cold and low,
Each like a corpse within its grave, until

> Thine azure sister of the spring shall blow
> Her clarion o'er the dreaming earth, and fill
> (Driving sweet buds like flocks to feed in air)
> With living hues and odors plain and hill."

Each of the five stanzas furnishes similar poetically cumulative passages, passages piled up by an insatiate mental liveliness, ever feeding itself on fresh beauties of its own begetting. Again, this poem is characteristic because through its musical tenderness there sounds an undertone of sadness; for to Shelley might be applied his own lines to the moon:—

> " Art thou pale for weariness
> Of climbing heaven, and gazing on the earth;
> Wandering companionless
> Among the stars that have a different birth?"

The "Ode to the West Wind" is not especially characteristic of Shelley because of the fineness of the mental fibre transparent in it, for that is visible in all that he wrote. One of the most richly endowed of men, Shelley was at the same time one of the most exquisitely organized. His sensibilities kept his life in a frequent tremor, and at times, when his imagination fastened upon images of terror, (and he was liable to morbid moods when such images were most congenial) his agony almost convulsed him. When a negotiation was opened with the manager of Covent Garden theatre to get "The Cenci" performed, with Miss O'Neil as Beatrice, Shelley exclaimed, "God forbid that I should see her play it! it would tear my nerves to pieces." This susceptibility made him recoil from the gross and robust and even from the palpable, while his intellectual subtlety, and his keen sense of the beautiful, ever tempted him into visionary fields, where he fashioned creatures who were largely absolved from the cumbersome conditions of earthly being. In a letter to one of his friends, Mr. Gisborne, he says, speaking of "Epipsychidion": "As to real flesh and blood, you know that I do not deal in those articles; you might as well go to a gin-shop for a leg of mutton as expect anything human or earthly from me." And that delicate resplendent creation, "The Witch of Atlas," is prefaced with six stanzas addressed to his wife, "on her objecting to the following poem, upon the score of its containing no human interest."

This objection cannot be made to "Prometheus Unbound." In conception, Shelley's Prometheus is grandly, intensely, human: in the execution its author yields to his overmastering ethereal bent, to his delight in expanding towards the unreal. By virtue of imaginative force Shelley holds his visionary figures firmly before his mind: to him they are distinct and lively, because the filaments that hold them issue from his own brain. But these fine filaments soon snap in the reader's mental grasp, and the figures float off into the impalpable. The figures are but phantasms; whereas it is only personages, humanly conditioned, that the reader can clasp long and close enough to feel and love them. In firm, pulse-thridded bodies the Divine Artist incarnates the ideas wherewith He wishes to rejoice man's sense of the beautiful. Shelley's incarnations lack the earthly element: he had too much nerve and not enough muscle. Hence in his "Prometheus Unbound," stamped as it is with greatness, the conception is not vividly accomplished. The Gods and Spirits and Impersonations that play around Prometheus have not enough red blood in their arteries. It is not a drama (Shelley entitles it a lyrical drama), but a dramatic lyric; that is, a self-rapt effusion, a soliloquy in dialogue rather than the objective, organic structure, whose essence is characterization, which a drama should properly be. The age was a lyrical age, so volcanic with change, with passion, with aspiration, were the tempers and thoughts of men.

In "The Cenci," Shelley plants himself firmly upon the earth, and weaves with the tremulous chords of human feeling, pages of passion and power that fill the reader with admiration. But the story is so revolting that the reader's imagination refuses to harbor it, and the protagonist of the drama is a monster so hideous as to be far out of the pale of human sympathy. Cenci, the father and husband, is a fiend, not a man: his doings spring not from human motives, they are the contortions of a blasé demon. Beside him Iago and Edmund are cherubs. To be sure, he was a reality, a reality engendered by the union of vice with despotism, of bestiality with superstition, which Rome presented (and only Rome could present) towards the end of the sixteenth century. But even the genius of Shelley cannot make Francesco Cenci a poetic reality, cannot make his criminal heart radiate a generic light, so far beneath the measure of the human scale is his moral deformity. So overwhelming are the deeds and personality of Cenci that the other personages are swamped in the mire of inhumanity through which he strides. All are so pale in the lurid glare of his demoniacal will, that there is little room for characterization, little for dramatic collision, and none for variety. Shelley has made the most of a subject to which he was drawn by that imaginative delight in excess which was one of his characteristics, and which, springing in him out of his very susceptibility to the beautiful, was liable to efface the beautiful with its devouring flame. In the preface to "The Cenci" he says: "The person who would treat such a subject must increase the ideal, and diminish the actual horror of the events, so that the pleasure which arises from the poetry which exists in these tempestuous sufferings and crimes may mitigate the pain of the contemplation of the moral deformity from which they spring." But not even his rare poetic gift and thoughtful art can subdue the horror, but it will envelop the reader and the personages in unpoetic gloom.

The Poems — now acknowledged to be among the most original and poetical in our language — that were published by Shelley before "The Cenci," met with no acceptance, and hardly with recognition; but "The Cenci" was at least partly appreciated, and Mrs. Shelley thought she saw in it the opening of a new mine, the working of which would further develop her husband's powers through the sympathy of the public. She endeavored to persuade him to repeat an experiment which had proved so successful; but Shelley, instead of yielding, wrote "The Witch of Atlas," the most exquisitely ideal and ethereal of his poems. In her note on "The Witch of Atlas," Mrs. Shelley says: "But my persuasions were vain; the mind could not be bent from its natural inclination. Shelley shrank instinctively from portraying human passion, with its mixture of good and evil, of disappointment and disquiet. Such opened again the wounds of his own heart; and he loved to shelter himself rather in the airiest flights of fancy, forgetting love and hate, and regret, and lost hope, in such imaginations as borrowed their hues from sunrise or sunset, from the yellow moonshine or paly twilight, from the aspect of the far ocean or the shadows of the woods, — which celebrated the singing of the winds among the pines, the flow of a murmuring stream, and the thousand harmonious sounds which Nature creates in her solitudes."

In my judgment not "Prometheus" or "The

Cenci," but "Adonais" is the masterpiece of Shelley. In it there is more of the poet Shelley, and more of the man Shelley, than in any other of his works; and the result is that Adonais is the finest elegy and one of the best poems in literature. Here we witness what lightnings can flash from the love-enkindled soul of a great poet. While writing the elegy of Keats, Shelley wrote that of himself, and this half-conscious aim deepened the beauty and the pathos of this transcendent poem. The four stanzas which directly relate to himself give the most brilliant and the most affecting portrait that was ever self-drawn: —

> "A pard-like spirit, beautiful and swift, —
> Who in another's fate now wept his own."

Who can read the sudden conclusion of this most touching, most tender, and most vivid portrait, without a thrill of awe?

In writing "Adonais," Shelley's best feelings, admiration of the admirable, poetic, and with it, personal sympathy for his great young rival, generous devotion, rightful wrath, were all keenly enlisted, and by the warmth of the occasion, and by the extraordinary demands made on him to celebrate a poet so unique, were fused into a glow, which, by the rare cunning of his hand, was fluently moulded into those pliant lustrous forms which only shape themselves in the sun of the most genial sense of the beautiful. Throughout all the fifty-five Spencerian stanzas there is the most easy and graceful and close and rapid interbraiding of emotion and thought. The poet is in his best mood. The personality of the theme, with his own affections and sorrows, hold his imagination closely to its duty. His cloud-cleaving tendency is controlled to concentrate the whole roused man upon the beloved theme. Through the action of his wrought faculties he exerts, with a copiousness even more lavish than elsewhere, the poetic power of compelling remote things into neighborhood, unlike, into similitude, scattered, into unity; but his illustrations and metaphors, even those brought from the farthest distances, are so apt and lively, that they cling to the thought before you, making it at once more clear and more compact. This high gift is used to put more life and character into the verse. In " Adonais" there is a stronger, steadier pulse than in any other of his poems.

XX.

SHAKESPEARE.

EVER behind appearances sparkles their mysterious source, appreciable only by spiritual insight; beneath all human doings sways their interior impulse, only fathomable by sympathy; behind, beneath these mysterious sources, these interior impulses, weighing them, measuring them, is the supernal source and mind which, in its perfect purity, repels the finest mote of soil, and in its plenary mercy, ordains the purification of the foulest. To feel the spring of this supreme dominance in all movements and conjunctions, is a prerogative of man, enjoyed in fullness only through the translucent susceptibility of the highest genial endowment. Through intuitive cognizance of eternal law, through healthfullest fellow-feeling with human desires, through intense joy in all manifestations of life (a token this of æsthetic genius), Shakespeare, with unexampled fidelity to the deep primary demands, presents pictures of being, doing, and suffering, in their infinite modes and varieties. Like his own Prospero, "his Art is of such power," he controls the stormiest motions of the soul, to play with them for his and our behoof. His gravest tragedies are an earnest sport with human passion; his lightest comedies are a playful conflict with human will.

The incorporation, through superhuman creative might, of thought and will in organic nature, is the daily wonder, ever renewed before our eyes: Idea, purpose, successfully, and therefore beautifully, realized in sensuous form and animated motion, the mysterious marriage which results in palpable being, the great unfathomable act of genesis, brought momently before us, to delight and teach, to unfold and quicken the eager faculties of our finite and infinite being! The most valid stroke of creative might — if without arrogance the same terms may be used — by the human mind in the realm of literature is the reproduction out of itself, the incorporation of men who, thus man-made, shall speak and do as God-made men speak and do, with a like elastic carriage, a like psychological absolute individuality. To utter warm clear sentiment under the rhythmic press of lyrical inspiration, is a high exercise of mental power, but higher than this single act is the compound act which gives to the utterance a broader significance, a more definite meaning, by grafting it into a brain-projected human being. Thereby the poetic strain becomes secondary to a concrete complex whole, and from being the all in all of the lyric, where it is the direct delivery of the poet, is subsidiary to a purpose higher than a personal effusion, and fitting its place as an exponent of character, gains both in brilliancy and breadth. Characterization, the creation of character, which can only be fully and permanently achieved through the vision and grasp of poetic power, and which implies a group of personages interacting one on the other in an organic series of doings, — characterization, in this æsthetic sense, is the loftiest literary achievement; for, in addition to many single literary qualifications, such as flexibility of expression, graphic gift, figurative faculty, imaginative intensity, it demands fullness of mental endowment, and a warmth that shall fuse all these qualities to the furtherance of a complex artistic end; and finally, as decisive equipment, it involves an intuitive insight into human nature combined with mimetic facility, so that the coördinated union of the above gifts may issue in rounded buoyant figures that shall move and speak like living men, only with a poetic transfiguration of soul through a poetic transparency of diction. The Germans are right to call Sterne and Cervantes poets; for in none of the epic or dramatic verse of Christendom, outside of Shakespeare, is there more plastic poetic fullness, more æsthetic truth, than in their immortal masterpieces.

To launch upon the sea of time a brain-built being so palpitating with soul, so mobile with individual life, that for centuries it keeps its freshness and wields its power amid the flesh and blood lords of reality, as do Macbeth and Don Quixote and my uncle Toby and Falstaff and Caliban, this proclaims a kinship with the invisible creative mind and mightiness, and exalts all humanity on the soaring wings of its sun-eyed poets. For the crowning mastership of characterization, Shakespeare, by his originality, his fidelity to nature, and his universality, takes the first place, being, as Coleridge with sympathetic insight so grandly says, a myriad-minded man.

In this multiplicity of gifts there is one, at once the subtlest and the broadest of all, with which Shakespeare among poets is uniquely portioned, and which, standing him always in good stead, is especially serviceable in his high dramatic function of characterization: I mean his sympathy with the super-earthly. Hereby, through emotional divination, he has range of the peopled world of the invisible. By all the abler among his critics and commentators, this gift has been noted; but has it been duly noted? Much more is it than one superadded faculty which enables Shakespeare to annex another Province to his immense Empire. A light it is, a vast Sun, in the heaven of his mind, sending illumination and warmth over the whole of that Empire. Through his gift of spiritual insight, through a belief like that of Socrates in his own spirituality, he is enabled to do what without such belief he could not do, namely, to overleap the gross and palpable of sense, and to grasp the key which opens the joyous realm where embodied act is not yet, but is ever hatching, the upper realm, whence the nobler sensibilities receive their polish, the realm mysterious, unfathomable, actively though impalpably above, around us, wherewith it is our immeasurable privilege to be in close, mystical, more or less conscious relation, and in imagination, nay, more than in imagination, to enter while still on earth. Herein Shakespeare reveled, sharpening by that higher light every weapon of his vast mental armory, growing visionary with a superlative visionariness, which empowered him to divine the thoughts and wills of men with a godlike clearness, and with a godlike sympathy and charitableness.

The distinctively human faculties in man being the spiritual and moral, only he who is largely endowed with these can figure to himself human beings in their wholeness. Had Shakespeare not been exceptionally fortified with the supreme sensibilities, not only would he not have been able to hatch in his mind and thence project the nobler among his personages, such as Kent, Vincentio, Duke of Vienna, Orlando, Antonio, Gonzalo, Imogen, Cordelia ; but none of his personages, not the lowest, would have moved before us with the fullness of being, the springiness of port, we now see in them. To measure anything, you must have in your thought a standard. To say that a man is six feet high, implies that you carry within you the conception of a foot. For moral measurement you need a moral standard ; that is, you must have within you, in full proportion, the faculties that distinctively constitute a human being, the spiritual and moral faculties. As, to judge of physical height, your own geometrical competence supplies you with a guage in a foot, so, to judge of moral height, your own spiritual competence must supply you with a moral foot. For lack of this moral foot, in unconfused sensation, it is, that moral judgments are often unsubstantial, and that such morally deformed idols are at times set up, to be temporarily worshipped.

Urged upward by interior want, and carrying with him, like cloud-cleaving Chimborazo, successive belts of fertility, the dramatist must reach this spiritual height, in order to obtain a clear survey of the wide diversified field where he desires to work. To this height Shakespeare rose with ease; nay, he habitually dwelt thereon; and hence there is an airy buoyancy in all his personages, even the most weighty, and in his pages so fine a light. The normal state of the poet, as such, is elation, elevation: when under the spell of the "vision and the faculty divine," he is lifted above himself, and this vision and faculty become more divine when sanctified by spiritual transfiguration. The poet's sight grows more transpiercing, his touch more luminous; he is more of a man and works from a higher plane of reality.

The sturdy realism of Shakespeare is but the solid basis to his lofty structures. Were his realism less earthy, he could not build so high. The grander the cathedral and the taller its spire, the more firmly must it grasp the earth with its foundations. Its foundations take their shape and proportions from the yet unreared grandeurs above them: within its stoutest folds the realism of Shakespeare feels his spiritualism. His consciousness of the coöperative activity and sympathetic helpfulness of the invisible powers, is a mystic and an animating influence which works into the texture of his personages, imparting to them some of that springiness which marks them as his. Shakespeare's delight in the marvelous is, of itself, an element of depth in him which tempers his whole view of life, and which even adds a vivacity to the least poetic of his dialogues. Shakespeare is a spiritual earthling, "a budded angel graft on clay," an Antæus, who draws strength from the earth; but unlike that giant son of the earth and sea, he loses not strength when lifted from the earth: he gains strength. As on his immense and minutely divided scale of characterization he ascends from the base to the top, the joyous laugh of the earthling becomes the benignant smile of the angel, the muscular grace of the athlete is changed to the wingéd puissance of a descending Michael. And, like a lucent atmosphere at midday, moulding the earth to joy and power, out of the sunny depths of Shakespeare's broad being come the breath and light of his moral nature, giving warmth and stability to details, and to the grander scenes and personages their wise significance and lasting worth.

XXI.

THE MERCHANT OF VENICE.

In the "Merchant of Venice" Shakespeare pits against each other two of the most irreconcilable opposites to be found on the fretful mart of human passions. Antonio, by lending money gratis, has hindered Shylock of half a million, which is daily to tap an artery of Shylock's life: that life is all run into love of gain. For this life-tapping, Shylock would, with his own hand, cut out the heart of Antonio.

In the conflicts of business and ambition two competitors often baffle one the other, without being unlike, at times indeed even from very likeness. But the intercrossings of such two would furnish a less capable subject for picturesque dramatic representation. In the case of Antonio and Shylock a deep moral difference underlies the mutual antagonism. Shakespeare dramatically needed the diversity, the oppugnancy, and so, as is his profound wont, he seconds his infallible artistic instinct with moral conditions, sinking, as nature does, into the inmost being the roots of the variegated flowers he has made to bloom on the surface. Had Antonio come to Venice as a visitor, and fallen but casually in contact with Shylock, and not as a constant counterworker, between the two, even had they both been Christians or both Jews, would have arisen a mutual instinctive repulsion, the one being generous, kindly, living much out of himself, carrying an open heart that is ever opening his purse: the other hard, morose from penuriousness, a griping usurer, who would use every man as so much capital, funded for his benefit, from which his own shrewdness was to draw dividends.

With his veracious perception of the actualities of life, and his masterly artistic handiness in harmonizing contrasts, Shakespeare at times includes in one frame Comedy and Tragedy. To tragedy death is not necessary; and there are catastrophes which to the victim would have been lightened by decease. The moral (in the high sense) may not demand the extinction even of a towering transgressor, and the proportions of Art may forbid it; but that to him death would have been, not a penalty, but a release, reveals a deeply tragic element. Such there is in the "Merchant of Venice." Had suicide been a crime to which Jews are addicted, instead of being one from which they recoil with peculiar aversion, Shylock might have turned his whetted knife upon himself with as much justification as do Brutus and Othello their swords; and, when overwhelmed by the sentence of the judge, and goaded by the taunts of the bystanders, he might have had the grim satisfaction of spattering with his blood the triumphant circle of Christian mockers.

Daily life offers many a group where, as in the "Merchant of Venice," in the midst of a light laughing company a tragic figure moves and errs and suffers, and where often his suffering casts as little of gloom as Shylock's did upon those about him. Hereby the tragic is deepened. Total refusal of sympathy, absolute isolation, aggravates the tragic condition, even though Shylock himself, from his unsympathetic habits, feels the isolation but partially.

Shylock is a peremptory representative, accredited by the sovereign, Shakespeare. The story of the Hebrew people, for two thousand years ever struck down, but never subdued, scorned, persecuted, but never weakened, never disheartened, this is the most loaded tragedy of History, a tragedy whose scenes are centuries, whose acts are the epochs of civilization, whose stage is the globe. Happily closed now is its last act, the ban against this remarkable people being lifted by the growth of moral culture in Christendom. The hard stern side in this excommunicated life of a people, Shakespeare has condensed into Shylock. Shylock leaves the court-room baffled, impoverished, cruelly mocked, but unbowed. His was not a spirit to be subjugated by man.

The heartlessness and levity of Jessica are to some a blemish on the beauty of this play. But Shakespeare, a rigorous realist, saw men and women as they are, idealizing each chosen specimen, not by smoothing its prominences with the false aim of academical impotence, but by unfolding each to its utmost in the light of poetic vision, — the only genuine idealization. By the absence of all sentiment in her smileless home, the natural superficiality of Jessica has been cultivated. Being unlike her father — as so many children are — the unlikeness, in the absence of all generous concession on his part (and children are particularly attached by generosity), grew to indifference to him, and, in the absence in her of earnestness of character, turns to dislike of his absorbing passion, and to frivolous contempt for its object. One of the curses of miserhood is its proneness to envelop its victim in a dark loneliness, even amid the household lights of affection. Around Shylock this gloom is deepened by the unfilial conduct of his only child, of which unfilial conduct his unparental conduct was partly the cause; while the unlikeness between the two heightens the play of contrasts, which is a characteristic of this brilliant drama.

XXII.

TAMING OF THE SHREW.

OUR world teems with materials for poetry. Wherever there is life, poetic aspects are to be won. Under every life-current which has depth to float a literary venture, there lie unrevealed treasures and gems, which only genius has the vision and the vigor to perceive and dive for, and which such genius joyfully seizes, and then holds up in the sun of admiration, dripping with beauty. To do this is the token of genial power, and if to the gift of poetic sensibility be added thoughtfulness and strength, it cannot but be done.

These fresh revelations of life and beauty may be called the nervous centres of a literary organism, the ganglia which concentrate and distribute motive force ; and according to their number, potency, and fineness, is the organic vitality of the work and its elevation, on the scale of æsthetic originality. At passages thus vitalized, the reader is arrested, to be warmed by the flame they kindle within him. Any one capable of poetic sympathy, can in a moment experience this animating warmth by opening "Hamlet," or "As You Like It." These two first occur to us because their subjects, being especially congenial to Shakespeare, they fill to its fullest his mind, which richly overflows, and deposits its wealth with as much ease and abundance as the Nile does its annual gift of fertility. You can hardly read twenty lines anywhere, without pausing to delight in some sparkling jewel set in the golden page. Now, of these gems of thought, sentiment, and expression, none are to be met with in the "Taming of the Shrew." Thence we conclude that this comedy is the work of the playwright Shakespeare, and not of the poet. Shakespeare, the greatest poet of the world, was also the greatest playwright. As the principal proprietor of a theatre, he made it one of his functions to keep his stage refreshed with new pieces. It was a dramatic age. Dramatic writers seem to have freely used the works of their predecessors, and even of their contemporaries. Collier thinks it is evident that, in writing the "Taming of the Shrew," Shakespeare made great use of a previous comedy called "Taming of *a* Shrew." A most skillful playwright, Shakespeare well knew how to tighten loose knots, to give a logical sequence to scenes, to put in touches characteristic or sprightly, and to bind the dialogue in that chain of vivacity, wrought in his wondrously vivid mind. To find a good subject ready dramatized, which by his manipulation would be made more buoyant and compact, was doubtless a godsend to the practical Shakespeare. He could thus, in two or three weeks, turn out a play that would draw as much into the treasury of the company, as one of his orginal dramas that cost him three or four months' work. That the "Taming of the Shrew" is only thus secondarily Shakespeare's, we infer from its almost total want in passages of poetic glow, such as in his other comedies shoot up, with more or less frequency, like jets of transparent fire.

A partial exception must be made for the speech of Catherine at the close of the play, the speech beginning "Fie, fie." Here is no occasion for glow; but what a sparkle there is of intellectual vivacity. This is all Shakespeare's. What a propontic flow in the current, showing, from its depth and volume, that there is a deep capacious sea behind it. And how thoroughly is the long speech saved from didactic tedium by the figurative luminousness in which its counsel is enwreathed.

XXIII.

THE TEMPEST.

Each play of Shakespeare has its character, as each of his personages has his or her individuality. When by Shakespeare a subject was taken up, its quality and the chief agents that give it consistence moulded the plan, and determined the nature and tone of the drama to be evolved. This seems to me his process. He did not select a subject directly for the purpose of exhibiting characteristics in individuals, or the effects of certain courses; but he set in motion the men and women who belong to a given circle of events, and, through their relations to one another, and to the end to which pointed their individualities, and the interplay of these, he shaped their combination into an organic whole. So versed was Shakespeare in the possibilities of human conjunctions and catastrophes, so deep in the confidence of the human heart, his imagination was so free and potent, that he had but to bring together the individuals who belonged to the chosen subject, and give them impulse from his own mighty being, and they, like their fellows in actual life, would work out a healthy moral, and, under the guidance of his æsthetic genius, present a rounded whole, as symmetrical in shape as it was lively in action and profound in import.

That this was the procedure of Shakespeare, is transparent on his page; and it was his because it is that of nature. In man the feelings are the primary power: the intellect is their instrument. The weal and life of the body is not more bound to the warmth of the heart that pulsates at its core, than is the personality of the man to his desires and aspirations: they build his character. The artist who would rival nature, must make the hearts of his personages beat sadly or joyfully, as the conditions may impose, but distinctly, energetically. For this he needs have within himself a warm, strong throb, that tunes itself with a ready love to the varied moods of humanity; and therewith a poetic ear that seizes the music in each. To construct characters in order to exhibit certain phases of doing or suffering, and with the understanding to plan all the movements and control them to a given end, this being counter to nature's method, will result, not in art but in artificiality, not in poetry, but in mechanism. The initiative is with the feelings, not with the intellect. In the drama, especially, the story growing out of the characters (in the epic the story governs the agents), these drive, so to speak, the events before them. For this, of course, they must be vigorously and warmly conceived, and so conjoined, so harmonized and contrasted, as to build by their action and reaction a whole at once picturesque and real. In the constructive function, in the handling of the materials furnished by the heart as well as those furnished by itself, the intellectual constituent of art finds one of its fields; and here the judgment of Shakespeare approves itself equal to his æsthetic susceptibility.

A deaf mute might give evidence of great intellect by the way in which he conducts himself and directs others; but besides action, which its name implies, the drama asks for talk. It is in the profoundness and keenness, the range and subtlety, the solidity and splendor of his talk, that Shakespeare exhibits again, in unequaled degree and harmony, the union of sensibility with intelligence. His talk is at once more natural and more ideal, at once more unprompted and more logically affiliated, than can elsewhere be read. The intellectual activity among his interlocutors is higher, more brilliant and better sustained than among any other talkers of whom we have record.

Of all Shakespeare's plays "The Tempest" may perhaps be deemed the most intellectual, in this sense, that having of course, a deep basis of feeling, the personages, their passions and aims, all coöperate to a triumphal pomp of intellectual power. In this wonderful poem the poet plays the god. He controls the elements, and creates living, speaking beings, the like of whom had not before been known on the earth. The raising and stilling of the storm, the mastery over the minds of the ship's inmates, this is the magnificent apparatus of the poem, symbolical of mental might. In Prospero is imaginatively displayed the power to be attained by intellectual culture and spiritual elevation, with self-devotion to high ends. But Caliban and Ariel are new creatures, not our fellows, like Iago and Imogen. They are sub- and super-humanities, sprung from a brain which, in the momentum of its imaginative sweep, and the intensity of its creative *vis*, swings beyond the known circle of nature, but, still intuitively obedient to her laws, gives birth to beings who are within the pale of nature, while outside that of earthly humanity.

Caliban, above the brutes, in that he has the use of speech and a broader intelligence, is yet below the upper class of them ; for Prospero says he will "take no print of goodness," and is one "whom stripes may move, not kindness ;" and Caliban himself declares that all the profit he has of language is that he "knows how to curse." Caliban is not *un*human, for he has no quality that human beings have not ; he is *de*human, that is, a being from whom the distinctively human has been subtracted. He wears in his head the precious jewel of intellect, but this is not irradiated by light from the spiritual and moral faculties, nor even by that from the upper reason, and hence it sparkles not, but is dimmed by fumes that are ever rising from the animal abyss. Fancy the horse and the dog endowed with as much understanding as Caliban to guide their selfishness, and with a corresponding capacity of speech ; then, instead of affectionate, faithful, subordinate servants, we should have in them self-seeking, treacherous, cruel rivals. All Caliban's joys and pains are of the flesh, and his fears do not reach beyond pinches and cramps. For the joy of drink he will make Stephano king, and be his slave. And here Caliban steps back into the pale of humanity. How many a man enacts Caliban, making himself the slave of appetite and passion, shutting out the upper light of which he has more or less within him (and of which poor Caliban had no glimmer), thus exiling himself from the beauties and beatitudes of life, and stifling his whole being into a self-built dungeon.

One of the preëminences of Shakespeare is this, that a trait or act, struck out of the individuality of the scene and personages, is discovered to be symbolical, at once specific and generic. Shakespeare did not say to himself, "Here is an occasion to embody a generality, to put forth in individual form what shall be a telling illustration of common human weakness." Not in the least. With his profound insight into being, with his vivacity of wit as well as of scenic movement, he drew Caliban to the life. An unbroken consanguinity binds into palpitating oneness the world of man, all its complexities and diversities; and such is the depth and fullness of Shakespeare's intuition, that a fidelity of detail like this lets a didactic type shine through itself. If you wish to show the grace of a beautiful young girl, you do not say to her, "My dear, walk across the room, that my friend may see how graceful you are;" that would somewhat mar your very purpose; but you send her across the room on an errand, and as she executes the small commission, she unconsciously displays a grace that would ravish the sense of beholding multitudes.

In the brain of Shakespeare, thoughts, the broadest and deepest, spring up spontaneously: they come to him he knows not how or whence, and gleaming out of upper spheres they yet fit an ordinary fact or motion, suddenly illuminating it, — thoughts high, subtle, imaginative, yet apt to the matter, abstractions that yet glow with a familiar light. A commonplace is sometimes enlivened by being turned by him into a far-reaching generality.

Shakespeare digs into the earth for Caliban. Caliban is steeped in sense. With roots deep under ground, he is but a stump of humanity, a growth suddenly truncated, and so without foliage or fruit. He has sensation and some understanding, but no aspiration, no conscience, no wide discourse of reason. Ariel springs from the other pole: in him we have a glimpse of what man will be when disburdened of his body. He is not unhuman: he is unbodied, and thence is superhuman only in the sense that he is above man in being exempt from the physical obstructions of flesh. The secret of the being and individuality both of Ariel and of Caliban lies, in the subtraction from normal human beings of some of their attributes. In Caliban the higher human, the spiritual and moral, have been subtracted; in Ariel, the wants and the cumbrance of the body. The one is the type of the earthy, material and gross, the other of the immaterial and subtile; and yet, neither has any quality or faculty not in human nature. No moral or intellectual quality, not in human nature, can be conceived by the mind of man. Any attempt to shape a being with extrahuman qualities, would end in nonsense. Soar as it will hundreds of millions of leagues into space, the imagination cannot exceed its humanity: to this it is bound by a thread that never snaps; at the utmost reaches of its flight, it will find no creature but of its creating.

The most of his subjects and plots, Shakespeare took from printed tales, or legends, or other plays. "The Tempest" is one of the few that has not been tracked to any of these sources. Collier turned over the leaves of every Italian novelist anterior to the age of Shakespeare, but found no trace of the incidents of "The Tempest." On the far confines of his imaginative range, Shakespeare may have espied some dim nucleus, which at once began to sparkle under his gaze, and which, fed on the stores of his invention, so throve, that it grew into "The Tempest." "The Tempest" is a translucent splendor, hung between earth and heaven, a glittering crystalline prism, through which from the Shakesperian sun shoot fiery beams, in their many-colored brilliancy, flashing onward forever, to glorify and animate the minds that are so blest as to come within their play. Here Shakespeare substantiates, with exceptional distinctness, his theory of poetic creation : —

> " The poet's eye in a fine frenzy rolling,
> Doth glance from heaven to earth, from earth to heaven,
> And as imagination bodies forth
> The forms of things unknown, the poet's pen
> Turns them to shapes, and gives to airy nothing
> A local habitation and a name ;"

and ever, even in the finest frenzy, keeping not only within the bounds of truth, but seizing and embodying the very essence and beauty of truth. This infallible truthfulness it is that constitutes Shakespeare's poetic greatness, his supreme literary elevation. None but the poet can know the whole truth, and when, as with Shakespeare, there is a unique completeness of endowment, the range is thereby so wide, so universal, that the poetic vision falls creatively on all kinds of incidents, interests, passions, casting illumination, and making the truth flash out, wherever it falls.

How Shakespeare clings to, hugs the matter in hand, with what a quickening virtue he transfuses himself into the scene and personages, so enlivening reality with poetic breath, that it seems more alive than actual fact, is in no scene that he drew more manifest than in the opening of "The Tempest," — the storm at sea brought before our eyes by the words and bearing of the crew and the passengers. The naturalness and fidelity conceal the art. In the next scene, where the storm is repeated in the report of it made to Prospero by his agent Ariel, Shakespeare out-Shakespeare's himself.

XXIV.

MACBETH.

BETWEEN Macbeth and his wife the murder of King Duncan was projected before the opening of the tragedy. In the last scene of Act I., when Macbeth, seemingly relenting of his bloody purpose, exclaims, in answer to Lady Macbeth's scornful reproaches,

"I dare do all that may become a man
Who dares do more is none,"

she rejoins,

"What beast was't, then,
That made you break this enterprise to me?
. . . . . Nor time, nor place
Did then adhere, and yet you would make both:
They've made themselves, and that their fitness now
Doth unmake you."

This cannot possibly refer to any interview between them since Macbeth's return home, for ever since his arrival, time and place *do* adhere, Macbeth having just preceded Duncan, who "coursed him at the heels," in their way to Inverness. Observe, in passing, the friendly, affectionate, and yet kingly greeting of Duncan to Lady Macbeth, and the delicate compliment when he tells her that he had purposed being before Macbeth, —

> " But he rides well,
> And his great love, sharp as his spur, hath holp him
> To his home before us."

This is a sample of that deep serene naturalness, which is one of the fascinations of Shakespeare, and at the same time of his breadth of treatment, his divine power of grasping a whole in all its complexity and the significance of its detail. This gentle confiding greeting of the king, what a foreground it is to the murder that is just behind it, blackening unseen the heart of the hostess he greets. Of the same kind is, at the opening of this scene, the speech of Banquo about "the temple-haunting martlet." The poetry is not all in the thought and exquisite execution of the passage; some of it is in putting such a passage just there.

The words, "nor time nor place did *then* adhere;" that is, when Macbeth first broke his project to Lady Macbeth, point necessarily to a period anterior to the opening scene of the play, ere Macbeth had gone to the field at the head of the king's forces. This is clear: these words can have no other meaning.

Now, go back to the third scene, and note the effect on Macbeth when Banquo and he are waylaid by the three Witches. These greet him with the triple title of Glamis, Cawdor, and king that shall be. What that effect is we learn from the exclamation of Banquo:—

> "Good sir, *why do you start*, and seem to fear
> Things that do sound so fair?"

Startled by the Witches' words, because they suddenly reveal the murderous secret in his bosom, Macbeth "seems rapt withal." While Banquo is questioning the hags, he recovers himself, and then the hopes that had made him conceive the murder return to him, freshened and deepened by the flattering disclosures of the witches. Eagerly he questions them, and is sorely disappointed when, without further speech, they vanish. The whole bearing of Macbeth denotes a foregone conclusion.

Now mark how he becomes still more deeply rapt when a few moments later he meets Rosse and Angus, sent by the king "to give thee from our royal master thanks," and they, greeting him as thane of Cawdor, so far confirm the outgivings of the Witches. Then we have that picture of the guilty self-questioning heart, one of those gorgeous passages, gold-embossed, and thicker studded than is usual even in Shakespeare, with sparkling jewels. Here he toys with the murder that is in his mind, though it makes his heart to knock at his ribs. A bloody gigantic crime does not, in a nature like Macbeth's, if in any nature, grow suddenly into ripeness for execution. The "supernatural soliciting" which at first shakes Macbeth, soon strengthens him, and the murderous plot, long before conceived, and which nearly slept, is reawakened, and reawakened into stronger light, as may be inferred from his speech in the next scene on leaving the king, who has just proclaimed Malcolm successor to the throne.

Let us now, outriding both Macbeth and King Duncan, reach Inverness in time to hear Lady Macbeth read the letter from her husband, and comment thereon. And first we ask, in the tenor and tone of that letter and in its brevity, is there not something taken for granted? But if the letter itself does not, surely the comment on it does, point to a foregone conclusion. Not a moment does she stop to consider the wonder of the revelation, but instantly on closing the letter, without pause, she exclaims : —

> "Glamis thou art, and Cawdor; and shalt be
> What thou art promised."

Most evidently the prospect here opened to her is no new one, but one which she was accustomed to look at. Had the thought of the crown been now first presented to her mind, how could it leap instantly, at one bound, to the great crime of assassination? This were out of nature. Moreover, how hardened by guilty imaginations, how steeped already in murder, by brooding on the nest of ambition, must be the heart that could prompt that appalling soliloquy, uttered the instant after she learns that Duncan is coming, and within five minutes after reading the letter : —

> "The raven himself is hoarse,
> That croaks the fatal entrance of Duncan
> Under my battlements."

And when, at the end of that soliloquy, Macbeth enters, with a burst of hellish joy she greets him, which he answers with, —

> "My dearest love,
> Duncan comes here to-night.
>
> *Lady Macbeth.*   And when goes hence?
> *Macbeth.*   To-morrow as he purposes.
> *Lady M.*   Oh never
> Shall sun that morrow see."

In the first Act, every time that Macbeth and Lady Macbeth appear, whether they be together, or alone, or in contact with others, each scene corroborates the preceding one in showing that the murder of the King was a project that had been entertained, and, in the minds of both, determined on, before the opening of the drama. When in the fifth scene, just after Lady Macbeth has read the letter, an attendant enters, and in answer to her inquiry, "What is your tidings?" answers, "The King comes here to night," her passionate exclamation, "Thou'rt mad to say it," is the outflashing of her joy that at once, within a few hours, by this happy circumstance, can be consummated the deed,

> "Which shall to all our nights and days to come
> Give solely sovereign sway and masterdom."

More in harmony is it with the habitual far-reaching forethought of Shakespeare, that this great tragedy, built on ambition, and the dark, more deliberate desires of mature life, should have its foundations laid solidly in the being of its two unflinching movers. By him effects are never presented unbacked by corresponding and sufficient causes. Shakespeare always sends down roots, strong and deep in proportion to the breadth and weight of the deeds they underlie and feed. The prophetic and loving interpreter of the human heart could not wrong and trifle with it, by making it improvise a gigantic crime.

This throwing of the murderous inception back beyond the time when the play opens, gives to the Witches their proper place. If Macbeth had not for some time carried the murder in his mind, then the seed was planted there by the greeting of the Witches when he first meets them on the heath, and they, bidden by him to speak, hail him as king that shall be. But that this was not the first seed, we know positively from Lady Macbeth's taunts in the seventh scene. And, had we not this convincing external evidence, ought we not to infer, from psychological causes, that it was not so? Would Shakespeare make a hag's prophetic hail the pivot upon which this whole tragic drama turns? More in consonance is it with the resources and the mysterious initiative of the human heart, to make the mind of Macbeth primary, and the Witches secondary in the forecasting of the murder. The Witches are a fantastic embodiment of the grosser human desires, of evil possibilities. Macbeth has conceived the murder, and these stand for the foul wishes, the black purposes that made him conceive it. The Witches are low, squalid, of the earth, most earthy, who burrow into the darkest and foulest fancies for ingredients for their hell-broth. They are an echo to the selfish aims of Macbeth, who is cajoled and flattered by them, just as we all are liable to be by carnal lusts and selfish wills and unhallowed ambitions. They suddenly fan into a blaze the fire that lay smouldering in Macbeth's heart. Our evil desires ever seize us in moments of weakness. That with all their earthiness they are unearthly, gives them a poetic efficacy, Shakespeare availing himself of the popular belief in evil spirits to make the instinct of the marvelous aid him in his high purpose.

The Witches open the tragedy with only a few lines, but these so significant that they are an overture to the whole play. Entering in thunder and lightning, they are met to appoint another meeting on the heath, "There to meet with Macbeth." In the thoughts of Macbeth is an embryo murder: their function is, so skillfully to feed the embryo, that it shall quickly come to maturity in act. Before vanishing, all the three unite in two lines indicative of their work and of the moral medium in which they do it, —

> " Fair is foul, and foul is fair :
> Hover through the fog and filthy air."

Macbeth, the stronger nature, has the initiative. He first broke the murder to his wife, as she avers in Scene 7 of Act I. The thought thus lodged in her mind, ambition and sympathy with her husband secretly nursed, imagination feeding it so succulently, that at the first vent offered, it rushes out full grown on receipt of the prophetic letter; and when, a few moments later, she learns that on that very night Duncan will be under her roof, so familiar and vivid had become the image, that mentally she commits the murder, and to her overwrought mind Duncan's death is as good as accomplished. More impulsive than Macbeth, holding the near and present more closely in her woman's intense one-sided view, while he takes a wider range and can weigh the *pros and cons*, she is enabled to spur him up to the mark when he falters.

In awful prominence and significance stands out the moral of this great poem. How the crime, once committed, swallows up the whole being of the two criminals : its absorbing omnipresence isolates each of them. In planning and doing the murder, what intimate union: each could then help the other. Now they can help each other no more; each is thrown upon the sheer individuality of each, left alone with his or her soul. Macbeth hardens, Lady Macbeth breaks. The masculine nature braces itself to tougher sinew, to bloodier doing; the feminine fibre relaxes and gives way. Macbeth keeps alone, restless, possessed as it were with the demon of murder. Even when talking with his wife he soliloquizes. This continuous introspection, this unquiet abstractedness of Macbeth, is an exhibition of Shakespeare's insight; of his æsthetic mastery, unsurpassed even by himself.

This tragedy is a sonorous sublime reverberation, from the mighty brain of Shakespeare, of the protesting cry of nature and conscience against murder, against

> "The deep damnation of his taking off."

With what fearful vividness is the crime depicted by the words and scenes which immediately precede the act, by the awful first effect on Macbeth of the commission, and by the accumulating train of terrible consequences! Before the dread features of the picture, the mind recoils in consternation.

XXV.

HAMLET.

There is ground for believing that Shakespeare worked at "Hamlet" during several years. Not that Shakespeare was for several years exclusively busy in writing "Hamlet;" but that the first draft was at intervals gradually matured and expanded until the last hand was put to it in 1604. Defective or questionable is, in most cases, external evidence as to the life and doings of Shakespeare; but accumulated internal evidence proves that the author of "Hamlet" wrought upon this play more than upon any other. "Hamlet" is the longest of his dramas, and at the same time the most compressed; its scenes are more numerous than in any other of his great tragedies, and yet, in none other will you find so many scenes throbbing with life and significance. While for animation, appositeness, progressiveness, the dialogue is throughout unsurpassed, there is a larger number of single speeches and soliloquies of Shakespearian depth and comprehensiveness. "Hamlet" contains more variety and more incident, together with a wider range of reason and experience, than any other drama ; more pregnant thoughts, more sentences of condensed wisdom, more tender buds of beauty to expand through all the seasons of time ; such profuseness in separable individualities of intellect and power, that the play would be overcharged with them, were there not in the substance out of which they spring, and which they beautify, such depth and breadth and warmth and meaning, that they are borne up buoyantly and gracefully, so that the pages look no more over-crowded than do the heavens with the countless stars they carry in their interminable spaces.

All these divers characteristics combine to prove that the greatest tragedy and poem of Shakespeare, and of literature, was the product of more than usual labor and deliberation, and that, should external evidence fail to make certain that Shakespeare had "Hamlet" in hand five or six years, we are authorized by these many internal marks, supported as they are by pretty well established dates, to infer that he wrought at it during at least three or four. It is the work upon which, more than upon any other, he concentrates himself, into which he puts more of himself, when at his best, and which thence becomes the most consummate product of his genius and of his judgment, the ripest and richest fruit of the most poetic human soul that ever was, the favorite of one who, of the priceless gifts of feeling and intellect had more to give than any other poet, and who here lavished them, pouring upon "Hamlet" in the ecstasy of creativeness, from the deeps of a profound soul and from the folds of a vast intellect, his fairest stores of thought and emotion.

The most necessary passions of the heart are loaded with inextinguishable fire, which may explode in lurid bursts, to rend and consume the possessor, or may burn smoothly, for the warmth and delight of his being. The story in "Hamlet" involves them all, all the great primary loves, the parental, the filial, the fraternal, the conjugal; and each and every one of them is baffled, wronged, wounded, scathed. The complicated violence done to one and all the chief personages, drawing on the poet's highest resources, swells to its utmost his creative power, and thence so fills with urgent life every part and page, that in "Hamlet" there are almost no merely conjunctive passages. The heat at the core carries the drama along with a momentum that keeps the continuity unrelaxed, thus rendering unnecessary those transition scenes, some of which can hardly be dispensed with even in the most compact and rapid dramatic evolution. Fullness of life there is always in Shakespeare: its brimming excess causes Hamlet to excel in what is a cardinal power of Shakespeare, and is a token of the finest and largest mental wealth, namely, the typical quality of thoughts and sentiments, and of personages, these combining vital individuality with generic breadth, to a degree almost surpassing even his usual achievement in compassing this great virtue of dramatic characterization.

Genuine idealization, that is, exaltation, through poetic insight and visionary grasp, with adherence to nature through fullest sympathy with all the promptings of the human heart, this, a characteristic of Shakespeare in all his dramatic work, especially in contrast with his dramatic contemporaries, is in his highest tragedies exhibited in its supreme phase. In Lear, Othello, Macbeth, Hamlet, there is what, without rant, might be called colossal idealization. The agonies undergone affect us so inordinately because, besides their deep truth to nature, the strong hearts that suffer throb with the pulse of the inordinate intellectual power imparted to them by the poet. If Hamlet did not say such great things he would long since have been dismissed from our intimacy. And the Ghost: with what a grand individuality he presents himself! A specific personality, what a towering figure he is.

Did it ever occur to the reader that in the greatest tragedy, the greatest poem of literature, a ghost, "the majesty of buried Denmark," is the principal personage? Prince Hamlet the chief actor in the scenes, the protagonist of the play, is the agent of the Ghost. Without the Ghost there had been no Hamlet. The Ghost not only reveals to Hamlet the murder, but prompts, nay, commands him to avenge it, and thus controls the whole action and development of the play. And note how Shakespeare shields this great ghost from the common charge against ghosts, that they are diseased subjectivities, the coinage of the seer's brain, not objective realities. He first brings him into the presence of the two sentinels, Bernardo and Marcellus, and makes him stalk *twice* before them. When these tell Horatio what they have seen, he answers, 'tis but their fantasy. Horatio, the calm, philosophical friend of the prince, chosen by Hamlet as his confidential intimate, because in him

"The blood and judgment are so well commingled,"

he was just the man to dissipate an illusion; and so, at the entreaty of Marcellus, he comes to the platform before the palace, with them, "to watch the minutes of the night." When there, as they seat themselves, that Marcellus may again "assail his ears" with what they two nights have seen, Horatio exclaims, "Tush, tush! 'Twill not appear." A few moments after he trembles, pale with fear and wonder, for the Ghost does appear; and as if to make assurance doubly sure, after an interval of five or six minutes, reënters, that all three, seeing him once more together, may harbor no doubt of his visible reality.

To Hamlet they report what they have seen, and nowhere in Shakespeare is there dialogue more vital and springy, nowhere more of that bound and rebound in the quick interchange of thought and word between the speakers, which is almost an exclusive property of Shakespeare. Hamlet earnestly prays them not to reveal "this sight." Secrecy could have been more surely attained by the Ghost's appearing to none but to Hamlet. But then the Ghost would have been chargeable with unsubstantiality, with unreality, with being a phantom of Hamlet's morbid troubled mind, and the ghostly element, now so impressive, would have been reduced in grandeur. Shakespeare was as consummate in artistic judgment as he was profound and true in æsthetic insight. When Horatio and the others are gone, Hamlet exclaims:—

"My father's spirit in arms! all is not well:
I doubt some foul play;"

thus giving voice to a strong irrepressible instinct of the universal human heart.

In the interview between the Ghost and Hamlet, what is first to be noted is the naturalness of the Ghost. To the sentinels and Horatio he had shown himself bodily as he was on earth, so that they knew him at sight. In his speech to Hamlet he presents himself alive with all the feelings of the earthly man still fresh upon him. Nor should we think harshly of him, that he prompts Hamlet to slay the adulterate incestuous beast who had murdered him. In this case to revenge was to do justice, which could in no other way be done. Hamlet beholds and listens to his father as he had known him two months before, only magnified, hallowed, by being transferred from the world of earth to the world of spirit. Nowhere in Shakespeare are words more alive than those uttered by the Ghost. It is as if there was more undiluted soul in them because the speaker is free of the hindrances of flesh. The picture of his state, the description of the seduction of the Queen, of the poisoning, how clear, how actual, how transparent, how concise. In Shakespeare — and it is one of the features of his greatness — the more intense the action of his mind, from the earnestness, warmth, and importance of the utterance, the more sure is there to be illustration, and remote illustration, which would be harmful arrestation, distracting intrusion, were there not such a glow and rapidity that the reader is helped and not hindered. Shakespeare's mind in highest action is so abounding, that it seems obliged to relieve itself from the pressure of thoughtful importunity. The increased momentum enlarges his orbit, and in his fiery course he whirls into his vortex new satellites. Thus when the Ghost hints at the secrets of his prison-house, and says, but that he is forbid to tell them, —

> "I could a tale unfold, whose lightest word
> Would harrow up thy soul, freeze thy young blood,
> Make thy two eyes, like stars, start from their spheres,
> Thy knotted and combined locks to part,
> And each particular hair to stand on end,
> *Like quills upon the fretful porcupine.*"

A few lines further Hamlet exclaims:—

> "Haste me to know it, that I, with wings as swift
> As meditation, or the thoughts of love,
> May sweep to my revenge."

Who but Shakespeare could, at such a moment, without disturbance, bring to the mind of the reader or listener thoughts of love? The Ghost answers:—

> "I find thee apt;
> *And duller should'st thou be than the fat weed
> That rots itself in ease on Lethe wharf,*
> Wouldst thou not stir in this."

Again, in depicting the seduction of the Queen, he pauses to lay before the reader one of those golden fruits of meditation, where thought and diction marry themselves in a cadency as of heavenly harps, which the language garners up as one of its brightest, weightiest treasures:—

> "But virtue, as it never will be moved,
> Though lewdness court it in a shape of heaven,
> So lust, though to a radiant angel link'd,
> Will sate itself in a celestial bed,
> And prey on garbage."

In the impartings of the Ghost to Hamlet,

there is a grandeur, a weightiness, a depth of earnestness, that befit the revealments of a wronged and murdered king.

The significance, the awakening impressiveness, the awe of the opening scene in "Hamlet," is in fullest keeping with the dread beauty, the lustrous depths of Shakespeare's foremost drama. What tingling life in every line! What a sudden bursting asunder of the veil between the world of sense and the world of spirit! In an instant we are translated to realms unearthly. We feel ourselves shuddering in the spectral mist which enfolds the Ghost, rapt away from earth to spheres untrodden. And the latter part of the second scene, what a vivid reproduction it is of the first!

The best commentators, even Goethe and Coleridge, insist that a general moral purpose presided at the creation of Hamlet. True it is that "We have here an oak planted in a costly vase, fit only to receive lovely flowers within its bosom; the roots spread and burst the vase." True, that there is in "Hamlet" a want of "balance between our attention to the objects of our senses and our meditation on the workings of our minds." But that Shakespeare wrote " Hamlet" to " exemplify the moral necessity" of such a balance, as Coleridge believes; or that he designed to show the effect of "a great deed enjoined on an inferior mind," as Goethe affirms, this seems to me to be making Shakespeare drive a shaft for the water of life into the plain of the mere understanding, whence no rich poetic current could gain momentum to gush; a procedure, is it not, — I ask in all deference to these two great poets and critics, — inconsistent with high æsthetic principles, principles which both of themselves have done much to establish by precept as by practice.

If the poet has not within him strong, healthy, moral sensibilities to dominate, half unconsciously, his whole work, all such purpose will be futile and will fail; and if these sensibilities be the staple of his being (as they must be in a great dramatic poet), the placing before himself such purpose will be, not merely superfluous, but obstructive and depressive, I might almost say, depletive.

To believe that Shakespeare had primarily in his mind a specific moral plan, through which he aimed in Hamlet to set forth the operation of certain mental compounds, were to make the clear-sighted poet put the cart before the horse.

This, it seems to me, is Shakespeare's procedure: He seized upon a theme pregnant with passion, capable of impressive presentation, and in unfolding the characters that give to such a theme its weight and purport, that make it indeed possible, he drew them or fed them out of his own profound warm intuitions, intuitions which had been cultivated and concreted by a sure active observation.

The lowest foundation on which the dramatic edifice is raised is not laid down beforehand, but lay ready in the depths of his own moral nature, in the same depths whence he drew the material for the construction; just as if you were to rear a solid gorgeous palace on a mountain of Carara, the compact marble, on which the base of the building would rest, furnishes the materials for the superstructure. In creating Hamlet Shakespeare had no special moral aim. In this, as in all his great tragedies, there is a deep sound moral, deeper, it may be, than in any other, there being in no other such portentous and manifold collisions, collisions in which the great poet shows his highest greatness by working them out in healthy harmony with providential wisdom. Hamlet was brought into being for Hamlet's own sake; and, breathing and moving before us in fresh palpitating life, his fellow men, by intimately consorting with him, can ever strengthen their moral as well as their intellectual being.

BREVITIES.

BREVITIES.

I.

SPIRITUAL, MORAL.

Our habitation, the Earth, is not self-subsisting; it moves in dependence on a fiery orb far distant: the Sun's light helps to feed the breath of our bodies. And shall we from the soil beneath our feet, from the dust into which our bodies dissolve, draw the breath of our souls? If millions of miles off is one of the chief sustainers of our flesh, where should we look for the source of the spirit we feel within us?

The ideas of eternity and infinity are innate in the human mind as attractions towards perfection, as indications and promises of incalculable progression and elevation.

Religion needs to be purified and steadied by culture and science.

We must be realists, not dreamers: we must found our convictions on facts, not on imaginations which are dreamlike. Nothing is nobler than facts. Facts are God's; imaginations are man's, and are only godlike, when they enfold coming or possible facts, or adorn existing ones.

Widely and kindly around us should we look as well as inwardly and upwardly, or we leave untenanted some of the heart's best chambers. Our breasts are large enough to entertain multitudes, and only when thus filled is our daily life a blessing.

The increasing delight in natural scenery is one of the proofs that man is growing nearer to God.

Possibly the mind cannot, in its most hopeful and its most far-reaching imaginations, outrun its capabilities. Were it a law of being that the most fabulous flowers, unfolded in the sun of the heart's warmest day-dreams, contain the seeds of substantial realities!

Just ideas are the only source of healthy

moral life. By them institutions are moulded, and to uphold institutions which ideas have outgrown, is to be destructive, not conservative. They are the best benefactors of their race who can discern and apply the deepest ideas; and thus the boldest reformer may be the truest conservative.

To see things as they are, one must have sympathy with the spirit of God, whence all things come. Then can be discerned to what degree there is remoteness from divine design, and thus actual conditions be rightly judged.

When you build selfishly, you build frailly. When your acts are hostile to the broad interests of your fellow-men, they are seed that will one day come up weeds, to choke your own harvest-field.

One has at times a desire to cast away all the petty memories and imaginations that cling around self, and to bound off into the empyrium of the Universal. Thus disencumbered, the Intellect and the Soul might make great discoveries. Is not this the secret of the clear-seeing glances of some of the mesmerized, that they are emancipated from the bonds of self, and for the time lifted out of the obscurities of fleshly life, into the translucent sphere of the disembodied?

Beliefs imply non-beliefs. Creeds are compounded mainly of negations. 1852.

Religion is the binding of the human mind to the invisible. A man is religious in proportion to the fullness wherewith he acknowledges this bond and to the degree in which his life conforms to the conditions implied in that acknowledgment.

Humanity is ever yearning and struggling for its higher life. Religion, love, truth, justice, liberty, these it instinctively seeks, gets first glimpses of, then views broader and less dim, then exalting convictions of the possibility of lifting its life into their dominion.

Most people are Christians by inheritance, not by acquisition; involuntary Christians, not Christians by will, individual feeling, and deed.

Sin came into the world, not through the

Devil, but through a nearer approach to God. It is darkness made visible by light. Before the light, no one knew of the darkness or felt it. Savages are not sinful. Sin is especially Christian, because the unfolding of the higher nature, through genuine Christianity, so raises the standard of life, that the lower nature is rebuked, as it was not before, becoming thus not only conscious of sin, but sinful; for until there was the higher light, the lower nature deserved not condemnation for its low deeds, these being then not measurable by the doer.

The wish to be free must not be confounded with a longing for exemption from restraint on appetite and willfulness, for such longing points downward; whereas, desire for freedom is a striving upward.

People selfishly ambitious think they are mounting a ladder; whereas, with every round they touch they get lower, each step carrying them further from the zenith of innocence.

Socrates denounced as the most fatal of conditions, "the conceit of knowledge without the reality."

A fruit of partial mental development, of ignorance, and somewhat of arrogance, a fruit of the tree of evil, still much eaten and relished, is, that men strive to guide themselves by their imaginations and inventions and conventions, instead of by Nature's laws and precepts; that is, by the shallow and mutable, the fragmentary and fugitive, instead of by the deep, the complete, the perennial. To pride, coupled with one-sidedness, much easier is it to imagine and presume than to discover and obey.

To found your faith on dogmas, conceptions, imaginations, instead of seeking truth through meditative investigation, with direct, earnest, conscientious search, is as though a mariner, instead of looking to the sun and stars, should strive to guide his ship by the clouds, which are but shifting exhalations from the very sea whereon he is tossed.

The simplicity and fewness of the physical elements wherewith, in the mineral, vegetable, and animal kingdoms, are compounded such countless varieties and degrees of life, prove the immense activity, resource, and sovereignty of the immaterial soul that wields and welds them.

True religion develops and deepens the conscience: it helps the heart both to be just and charitable.

Think of the exultation, tinged with a blush, there must be in the thought of one, a purified spirit, who looks back to earth to see there her name still linked to shame for deeds done in the flesh, which now her soul has repented of and purged away.

A lively sense of moral responsibility necessarily involves dutifulness to our fellow-men, and thence dependence on them, and is the firmest, deepest, broadest, most indispensable foundation for individual worth and social well-being.

Some people seem to think that all religion is shut up in churches. They might as reasonably believe that all vital air is shut up in parlors and chambers. What is so shut up soon gets foul, and, unless daily refreshed from the great natural reservoir, breeds disease and death.

The dog and the elephant are finitely circumscribed: they have no above and beyond. To live consciously amid the unseen and the unknown is the sublime privilege of man.

The attempt to *know* the Infinite, were a most futile misdirection of human faculties. As well attempt to perceive melodious sounds by the eye. Ideas of God come to us only through our emotions. Reason about what the emotions furnish we can profitably; but most unprofitable is the attempt by reason to weigh, define, and fathom what, being purely objects of emotion, can neither be defined nor fathomed.

Only when religious organizations are sources of intellectual culture and schools of instruction, do they a high service. A priest or minister of religion who is a dullard is of no account. The religious sentiment, being innate in man, manifests itself in all times and latitudes; but that its spirituality have scope it needs union with intellect and moral thought.

The power of the Bible is in its cordiality.

Shame is a veil thrown by the spiritual man over the animal man.

In early manhood some souls get locked up in ecclesiastical prisons, and the bolts rusting from the stale exhalations of stagnant theologies, the prisoners languish their lives out in spiritual chains.

Curs yelp at the sage as loudly as at the thief.

A pity when men do not grow into light as they grow old, but mostly grope in a still colder darkness.

No man who has a humane spirit, and leads a practical life, but will be often an uncrucified martyr, so saddened will he be, and sometimes excruciated by the vice and suffering and anguish and injustice and inhumanity around him ; unless, like Oberlin, he withdraws into the mountains amid a primitive people, and thus restricts his life and his experience.

The most fearful thing in life is the dread of death ; and this dread which theologies have fostered, is getting dispelled by Spiritualism.

We do not value, or even know, our inward

worth and sacredness: we waste ourselves on the outward.

Truth is a fruit that ever hangs ripening above us, expectant of our harvesting.

There are words and doings so intensely natural that they seem supernatural.

The dear ones gone are living links between us and heaven.

Think of the interminable lengths of human relations in time and space!

The glass is not worn out by your looking through it; nor is the soul.

Some men despair of the future; as if God, Nature, and Humanity were at the end of their tether; as if Providence had in its hand no more trumps.

In the Stoic philosophy Physics and Theology, or the study of the nature of things and the divine government of the Universe, went wisely together. Nature, — including in the term all that is cognizable by man, all physical, physiological, intellectual, psychical phenomena and laws, — Nature, in this full sense, is the Book of God, a bible direct from his hand, not liable to erasure, interpolation, or falsification. Our printed Bible is at second hand, through human organs, colored by the minds through which the revelations passed. Nature is an ever-present, daily, living, teeming, beautiful, significant, prolific, incorruptible revelation.

Oh, the curse of egotism, the deadly poison of self-seeking! A man is but the fraction of a man, until he goes out of himself.

Creation is goodness in its most forceful phasis. To create is to be beneficent: to bring into being, to launch upon the boundless sea of life, is the highest act of love. Thence, to do acts of love, genuine acts, is to be creative. Every, even the smallest kindness we do, is to work in harmony with, and in furtherance of, the divine creative energy.

I have on my mind an image, brought from far childhood, of a rude woodcut, representing a man half buried in the ground and struggling to get out. What was typified I cannot recall; but I am reminded of this picture by contrast, when I see people and communities half buried in animalism and conventionalism, who are not struggling to get out, but sit in as much contentment as people can sit who, with all their self-satisfaction, can never utterly stifle the moanings of the soul in its slavery.

A man's well-being is only then attained when he is in upward movement, the human organization being happily such that his tendency and necessity is, to be always changing, and, when in sound condition, to be always ascending.

The maxims of La Rochefoucauld are an impertinence to humanity.

The Bible is the wisest companion and guide that men have had in their darkened pathways through the ages. Beheld in comparison with the consecrated books of other Peoples, the Bible glistens. That men are now getting dissatisfied with much of it, and have begun to criticize it, is a sign that their path is less dark.

So late as the fifth century the heathen gods and Jesus were publicly adored in the same town. In the Sermon on the Mount is there any word about adoration, or about worship by the help of priests? The whole system of worship as now almost universally practiced in Christendom is of heathen origin. Is there not, in formal outward worship, an inevitable materialism, which arrests and absorbs spirituality.

Sir Thomas Browne calls the soul, "that translated divinity and colony of God."

The greatest gift to man, from God the giver, is love of truth.

It is because the life beyond the earth-life is of such immeasurable importance to man, that in his less developed stages he has been a prey to priestcraft. Priests, pretending to be the privileged interpreters of the divine, have made man believe that they hold the keys to the passage which leads to the mysterious future.

To purge the world of lies, this is the great achievement of progress, — progress being the effort of life to shelter itself under more and more truth. Theology, being based, not on high facts and absolute truth, but on man's fancies and changeful opinions and even prejudices, has done much, in its obstinate limitations, to keep men false. Church-votaries it has filled with self-righteousness and hypocrisy.

Confucius said: "An ocean of invisible intelligences surrounds us."

With semi-animal imaginations people figure up a sum which they call Deity, and then strive to believe that their deepest, noblest thoughts and emotions, and their whole being, are but fractions of this sum. 'Tis as though they were to stretch into the air a fantastic apparatus of wheels and pulleys, and to strive therewith to sway the motion of the earth. The only strength such an apparatus could have would come from the earth whereon it rests. Out of yourself you stretch wires towards Heaven, and then you persuade yourselves that they have been stretched from Heaven towards you; and by the pulling of these wires you would direct your life. Who are the wire-pullers is as easy here to discern as in political jugglery. The proceeding is contrary to eternal law: it is an attempt to subordinate dynamics to mechanics.

The one only thing that is is *truth:* whatever is not true is not.

How were it if Copernicus, or some other, had not upset the Ptolemaic misbelief about the solar system, to which the Church held so obstinately? Goethe looked upon the discovery of the revolution of the Earth round the Sun as the greatest, most sublime, ever made by man; as boundless as beneficent in its consequences.

The men who lead a second, inner, higher life are they who fecundate their age and the minds of other men in after ages. Only from this inner perennial spring flow streams of spiritual and intellectual wealth to enrich mankind with deposits from their currents.

II.

LITERARY, ÆSTHETICAL.

POETRY is not put into verse to please the ear: it is in verse because it is the offspring of a spirit akin to that which dwells ever in hearing of the music of the spheres. To poetry, rhythm is as natural as symmetry to a beautiful face. Genuine verse delights the capable ear, because, like the voice of childhood or of woman, it is in itself delightful. Why does the setting sun, a lively landscape, a worthy deed, give enjoyment? Because they speak to, and are in harmony with, our higher being; and so is poetry, and therefore it too gives enjoyment. But to say, that the object of poetry is to please, ranks it with the shallow presentations of the showman.

The Poet is an apostle of truth; and the false can never be poetry.

A good book is a distillation.

In poetry much of the meaning is conveyed by the sound. Transpose the words of a fine passage, and you impair its import.

In the style of Shakespeare there is oceanic undulation. In that of Corneille and Racine the surface is level, or if broken, it is not with billows.

A sonnet should be like a spring, clear and deep in proportion to its surface; and like a whirlpool, in a certain silent self-involved movement.

Shakespeare's words, when boldest and richest, are but ambassadors, behind whom there is a greater than themselves: Racine's and Alfieri's, though not so erect and gorgeous, are the kings themselves; they leave nothing untold, and give no impulse to the imagination.

Good rhetoric is a good thing in a good cause.

Rhymes should sit as lightly on verse as flowers on plants.

In English Prose where is there a diction so copious, apt, forceful as Carlyle's, at once so transparent with poetic light and so compact with a home-driving, idiomatic solidity, doing the errand of a thoughtful fervent nature with such fullness and emphasis?

Goethe goes out of himself into the being of nature and of other men: Wordsworth takes their being up into himself. These two poets illustrate sharply the difference between the *objective* and the *subjective*.

In the plainest of Wordsworth's many hundred sonnets there is more or less of the fragrance of high humanity.

Some of Wordsworth's poetry is, as his person was, too gaunt: it wants a fuller clothing of flesh.

A fit ideal embodiment of the Artist were a countenance upraised, beaming, eager, joyful, moulded with somewhat of feminine mobility.

Thought is ever unfolding: a good thinker keeps thinking.

To write a good literary book, whatever the subject, requires the "instinct of the beautiful."

Music is a marriage of the sensual with the spiritual: each is merged in the other. In perfect harmony there will be neither sensual nor spiritual, but the two will be made one in the fullness of life and purity.

We talk of this man's style and that man's, when, rightly speaking, neither of them has a style. Style implies a substantial body of self-evolved thought. Now, from so few minds come fresh emanations, that most writings are but old matter re-worded, current thought re-dressed. Each one's individual mode of re-wording and re-dressing is, and should be called, his *manner*, not his *style*. In Writing as in Painting, every man, the weakest as well as the strongest, must have a manner; but few can have a style. 1852.

I write the opinion with diffidence, but to me it seems that Italian poetry wants depth: its roots are not sunk in the soil: too much of it is but ornamented versification. Dante borrows from or imitates the Latin poets on every page. Petrarca's sonnets are as much an embodiment of what is called Platonic love as of passion for Laura. In Ariosto there is abundant fancy, but little poetic imagination. Alfieri's horizon is definite and earthly; it does not stretch into the infinite.

In the "Divina Comedia," the supernatural is not the framework merely of the Poem, it is the chief constituent of its essence. In the plaint of Francesca, in the beatitudes of Beatrice, pathos and beauty are emblazoned by the glow from a supersolar sphere. To show them, and a crowd of other personages, alive in transterrestrial being, throbbing with human feelings, demands a poet of sensibilities rich and tender, and of graphic intellect. But the launching of the whole beyond the earth-orbit, this it is that sustains it and makes it poetical as a whole and in its multifarious details. As narrative of man's sorrows and joys while in the flesh, it were prosaic. The super-earthly firmament lends light to the picture. But for the supernal plane whereon every line rolls, and to which the reader is imaginatively lifted, the words, just as they stand, would be flat and opaque in nineteen lines out of twenty.

The men of letters who are contemporaneously overrated, are the men of talent. Men of genius are liable not to be rated high enough in their generation. More accurate were it to say, that men of genius can be appreciated only by the few; while men of talent, being within reach of the many, are by them self-complacently exaggerated.

The vice of written histories is, that they are not History.

Goethe's profound title to his Autobiography, "Dichtung und Wahrheit," Imagination and Truth, would be appropriate for every biography, memoir, or history that ever was written.

Only the men who can originate are fully competent judges of what has been originated and done. Talent alone can never make a thorough critic. For that enough genius is needed to sympathize with genius.

A beautiful face is fascinating more by what it promises than by what it is. To the beholder corporeal beauty suggests all other beauty.

When first gazing on a beautiful person, what an impertinence were a thought of his or her moral deformity. On the physical basis imagination builds all other perfections.

A fictitious story, to be worth attention, should have a heart in it, and be artfully unfolded, and be supported, not on slender temporary timbers, but on solid arches of thought and imagination.

True Art helps and upholds the higher part of our nature: the lower being aggressive, needs check not spur. The ideal involves elevation through emotion; and emotion, being caused by a stir of the unselfish feelings, is always purifying. There is no Art without some breath of the ideal.

Poetry is the aromatic essence of life.

The imagination unites, orbs, several into one: the fancy divides and individualizes.

Thackeray and Dickens are so popular in England (and America?) on account of their thoroughly English natures, both being somewhat material and matter-of-fact, with a strong earthy flavor, and not finely imaginative.

Some minds are filters of other men's thoughts. They add nothing: they clarify what passes through their pens.

The motion of a deciduous cypress illustrates grace. Under a breeze the whole stem sways, animating every branch and spray with its own slow, stately, reserved movement, which seems to come from within.

To those critics who, totally lacking poetic imagination, yet pretend to a fine ear in poetry, may be applied a "thought" of Pascal: "On ne consulte que l'oreille, parcequ'on manque de cœur." And the want of soul makes the ear untrustworthy.

The sun-fired focus of a lens consumes paper or wood, but falling on a diamond, makes it sparkle the more. So with books, under the focus of genuine criticism.

Some poets one outgrows. Scott, Moore, Campbell, even Byron, if I read them now at all, I read momentarily. Their verse is not deep enough, not compact enough with mind, that in maturer years we be enlightened by it, and thence delighted with it. Beneath the web of incident and sentiment and passion, there is not warp enough of thought. Their pages are not enduringly suggestive. Dimmed to the eye of manhood is the brilliancy they shone in to the eye of youth. Their words are too little swollen from inward sources of sensibility that many lines should glisten with inexhaustible meaning, as in Wordsworth, Coleridge, Shelley. Keats died at twenty-five, and yet, to men past sixty he is fresh, freshening.

There are writers whose minds have no horizon: they do not let you see far, but keep your looks on near objects and on bounded prospects.

The best business of the poet is, to spin golden threads between earth and heaven.

No high literature can be produced or enjoyed but through delight in the true and the beautiful.

A great function of sensibility to the beautiful is, to be ever prompting a better, finer something not yet attained.

In theatric pieces common reality is everywhere copied ; hence flatness, and a necessity for accidents and extravagances, monstrosities even, to keep alive a sensuous attention. The Stage should always be ideal, in the sense that Shakespeare is ideal, that is, it should present the real exalted, spiritualized. Literal reproduction is low literature.

To the poet who is a thinker, to Wordsworth or Goethe or Shelley or Dante or Coleridge, metaphysical speculation, if he chooses to give in to it, is an unbending. Nothing draws upon the mental life like poetic creation.

One of the great disappointments in Literature is the coming upon the stars which show that the " Hyperion " of Keats is a fragment.

Shelley balloons it too much. He ascends easily, gracefully, and then is swayed by scented breezes from an exuberant imagination. It had been a gain could he oftener have dipped his mind deeper into the core of common things. He has too much elevation and not enough depth,—that is, not enough depth for *his* elevation.

An elderly poet, who has written chiefly out of his fancy and memory, and whose borrowings are not the worst of him, may be called an exhausted receiver.

The pages of some writers, like the discourse of some men, are prickly with self-conceit.

The first question to ask of a new book is— Does it give out new light? Are novel aspects won from old things? or, better still, is it racy with original views and principles?

Men who have not the mental largeness or spiritual momentum to go out of themselves, who cannot lift them reverently towards a greater than themselves, are liable, if intellectual, to be pantheists. By this opaque doctrine they are blinded to believe that they are a part of the Godhead, in the sense of being identical with Deity. Whatever they may think, they do but shut themselves into themselves, and therein see but themselves, and that darkly.

Anybody, with a pen in his hand, can write about a given subject : few can write into it.

Common sense should lie at the bottom of all enterprizes, the literary and poetical as well as the practical and scientific. Good sense is the ballast of genius ; nay, we might say, it is the cargo itself out of which genius works its successes.

To move on a high plane of sentiment and thought is a privilege of the personages of Shakespeare.

"Great thoughts come from the heart," says Vauvenargues.

Hardly anywhere have we education, properly speaking ; that is, an educing, a drawing out of the inward powers. We teach, we do not educate ; we inculcate, we do not unfold ; we shape more than we dilate.

By the rarely beautiful we are subdued, overpowered. In its glow we feel that there might be a degree of it on which we could not look: the mind would be smitten and blasted, as the body may be by a flash of physical lightning.

In order to give life to their straight lines, the Greeks drew them with the hand and not with a rule.

That is never a bad book which sets us to thinking; but that is which makes us feel wrongly.

Capacity of admiration, delight in admiration, is essential to the poet. When a poet ceases to be capable of admiration, he ceases to be a poet.

How much is from himself, and how much has he drawn from others — these are cardinal questions to be put to him who offers us a new page of literature. Of genuine literature freshness is the first quality. Along the lines should glisten a life imparted from the writer's inmost.

Analysis is decomposition and, unchecked, leads to nullity. In literature as well as science the synthetic force must counteract and balance the analytic.

So much verse is but embroidery; some wrought with golden threads, some with silver, but mostly with fading silk.

To put novels into the hands of the young is to fire the feelings through the imagination, which is like applying a match to the combustible materials you have collected for building a costly mansion.

In the lines of genuine poetry is ever perceptible the undulation inherent in life; and this however calm may look the exterior. So much verse being drapery, thrown with more or less art over a subject, there is in such none of that spring which only issues from interior movement.

To deal competently with a subject the writer must first get into its centre, so as to write from within it.

To the brain-fibre of literary men may be applied the distinctive epithets of the cotton-planter to his crop: short staple, medium, long staple.

Metaphors give spring and buoyancy to sentences, widen the horizon, let in light and air, draw the reader from too close a look on the ground before him, and when fresh and appropriate, lift the style at once into significance and luminousness.

A profound characteristic of divine government is the *indirect* means for compassing ends. To work by indirection is to work after the method of Providence. If to the selfish and the sensual I hold out immortality as a threat, I abuse it and misuse them: if through persuasion of its reality I bring their minds into a broader, freer state, I use it wisely and serve them. Art acts indirectly: it lifts the mind to a higher mood, and out of that springs the will and the power to do higher things.

Kant has a fine definition of the *naif:* "Nature putting Art to shame."

To say a good thing fitly, demands some poetic gift.

When you come upon a poetic sparkle you feel suddenly illuminated.

So much verse has shallow roots.

Poems differ much one from the other in what may be termed their specific gravity. For example, "The Burial of Sir John Moore at Corunna" has much more specific gravity than Campbell's "Battle of the Baltic."

Profoundly does Sir Egerton Brydges say: "There is implanted in the poet a spiritual being, which adds to the material world another creation invisible to vulgar eyes."

The description of Valeria by Coriolanus vividly exemplifies *poetic* imagination:—

>"Chaste as the icicle,
That's curded by the frost from purest snow,
And hangs on Dian's temple."

The drama, the poetic drama, clings closest to the heart; clips the man in its arms; is one degree less removed from the inmost.

Deep in the personality of the poet a poem

must have its roots, in a soil rich and mellow. Out of himself it must come, not out of his memory and fancy.

A poem demands roundness, a circular completeness in itself and in its parts, such organic fullness that there be naught but lines like those of the egg, all representing a living rotundity, a palpitating unity.

The moral of a poem should lie at the bottom of it, like the stones of a limpid stream. Looking intently, you see the stones, solid and still, the basic boundary of the stream. By them its pureness is preserved when the water courses rapidly; for were they not there, the forceful rush would stir the mud beneath, making the whole current turbid.

At the core of all verse there should be emotion, sentiment, or however may be called the offspring of healthful sensibility. The intellectual part of poetry should be but the transparent medium through which you are enabled to behold the treasures of feeling, as you gaze at precious solid things that lie at the bottom of clear water.

Utterance is the one end of a poetic thought, whose other end is deep in the soul of the poet, — at times so deep that he himself knows not where it ends. To take in the full meaning and beauty of such verse, the reader must follow it into the depths whence it shoots. Thence it is that the best poetry is slow to be recognized.

Poetic genius is a lively soul uttering itself through the organ of the beautiful.

Tennyson is one of the poets who, like Virgil, have more art than inspiration.

Goethe says, there is poetry which is null without being bad; null, because it has in it no fresh substance; and not bad, because the writer had, from familiarity with genuine masters, fine forms ever present to his mind.

It is safe to judge a writer by the company he keeps; that is, the thoughts he habitually entertains, and the authors he likes most to hold communion with.

That only is literature, in the refined sense,

which continues to be read : it so continues, because it embodies in the best form the best thoughts of the best men.

A man's mental tools have their finest edge put upon them by his sensibility to the beautiful. Many subjects he cannot penetrate at all without this sensibility, and into all he strikes the deeper for its edge.

The poet deals with the new, with what is freshly formed and forming within him ; the man of understanding with what is old, finished, hardened.

In the best literary work there is a great deal of spiritual joinery.

Art implies fine nature well tilled : with all your tending you cannot have exquisite flowers without good soil.

In the fervor of work Shakespeare had little thought of style ; writing out of a mind so full and so poetical, style was a power inseparable from his utterance. When he had written a scene or act he went over it, and then he had a thought of style, and made changes to give additional depth, light, buoyancy.

Sense of beauty does not gild the variegated worlds of thought, feeling, and perception; for gilding is too shallow, artificial, and perishable a process to typify the action of this great sensibility. It illuminates with unexpected joy some of the darkest throes of human movement, suddenly lights up with hopeful hue thoughts and deeds that a moment before were black with gloom, like mountain-peaks, emerged from storms, suddenly shone upon by the calm beautifying sun.

In Hallam's " Literature of Europe during the Fifteenth, Sixteenth, and Seventeenth Centuries," there is shown a sound, but not a fine, still less an active sensibility. Now an active sensibility is one — might it not be said the chief one? — of the pre-requisites for a good style.

Personages, characters, make a drama, and to make it they must be marked individualities, not mere labeled mouth-pieces.

Out of the extemporaneous flow of his mental abundance, Shakespeare enriches barrennesses, peoples wildernesses.

In writing, especially in poetry, the transitions are vital ; and most vital are the transitional leaps, which only genius can make.

In writing, how few styles have nerve and sensibility ; without these the best and highest style is not reached.

In some minds there are no recesses, where stores, often unconscious stores, lie waiting for their occasions.

Poetry without personality is thin. To bring forth his personages, the mind of Shakespeare was big with humanity. When Shakespeare had dramatically given birth, his being was enlarged ; he felt himself reëmpowered by the soul wherewith he had imbued his creation.

Poetry needs primarily the sequence of feeling ; and this sequence only flows from a full inward spring.

That there be a poem, strictly a poem, the subject should have a rooted steadiness, an internal repose, a generic solidity. "Aurora Leigh" and "The Gypsey," works of poetic genius though they be, are too tremulous with feeling, too unsteady with superficial incident. They are like a fine head sculptured out of conglomerate; the vision is confused by the want of unity and purity of surface, and the lines and outline are broken by the shifting variety in color.

The scholastic, mediæval system of educating through Greek and Latin, is the superficial, hollow system. Little more than a thin shell is imparted. The learners get no Sophocles, no Virgil; no, not one of them in twenty. They do not even get possession, practically and permanently, of the languages in which Sophocles and Virgil wrote. A teaching not superficial, but penetrative and procreative, would be to take up Milton or Wordsworth, and lay his language, his thought, his poetry, open to the hearer. Aye, but who can do this? How many professors in all our colleges and universities (so called) can deal in thoughts, ideas, expression and poetry, with critical discernment and mastery? But such teachers, teachers of literary insight and range, are just what are wanted in our higher institutions of education, and these institutions, wanting such teachers, are but nominally high.

The first requisite for simplicity of thought and style, is truth of feeling.

There is no best poetry without flights, without steady, sinewy soaring up to plains where gleam lights spiritual, that flash new meaning upon life.

In poetic creation the feelings use the intellect as their instrument; in poetic composition the intellect uses the feelings. Schiller was less of a creator than Goethe, and more of a poetic composer.

Whatever he handles, the true poet illuminates with his own soul.

Consider what goes into the making of one of Shakespeare's best similes or metaphors. To follow these sunlit wings to their teeming nest, there needs a kindred imaginative nimbleness.

In Wordsworth there is a poetic thoughtfulness, and, in his higher moods, the polished compactness that results from this fine rare combination. His best passages have the smoothness and elasticity and roundness of an ivory ball.

From the pen of none but a great meditative poet, could have come this profound thought of Wordsworth:—

> "Instruct them how the mind of man becomes
> A thousand times more beautiful than the earth
> On which he dwells."

Rhythmic flow, in some form, is part of the incarnation of poetry.

Any feeling which can be lifted high enough to be married to emotion, becomes thereby fit for poetic use. Emotion results from movement in the higher, more generic feelings.

They can hardly be called poets who have neither intellectual vivacity nor poetic glow enough to make flexible and distensive the bonds of words in which it is necessary to bind sentiment and thought.

The best of poetry is the mood it creates; and herein the spiritually-minded poets are the most privileged. Not only do they tune the reader to a higher mood, but through his happy memory of this condition, they draw him back to their page, which, embalming in fit melody the better life of the mind, grows never stale.

Poetic ornamentation, like the relief on a teapot, is hollow.

Having no rhythm in their thoughts, the poetically unimaginative try to make up for this cardinal want with metrical smoothness; but smoothness causes no radiance, that proceeding only from internal self-kindled fire; and radiance attests poetry. In their verse there is no sign of bemastered emotion, of full feeling wrought in its plastic warmth into graceful strength.

For a word that is prosaic you can only get a poetic by going farther and deeper.

Under the touch of warm active thought words are malleable. Thought is their commander, and not only enranks them, but, like a Cæsar into his soldiers, breathes into them its own spirit, so that the dull become lively, and the weak strong.

By poetic imagination it is that recondite relations are detected.

In the poetically imaginative stroke many rays flash together from various quarters upon a single point, making that point to sparkle with concentrated lustre.

The composer says, " Here is a proper place for a figure," and straightway he manufactures one; but figures, to do their duty of enlivening while they illustrate, should flame up out of the warm air that has just been liberated by the busy play of thought. In poetry the *play* of thought is everything.

Of a truth, says Goethe, the head takes in no work of Art but in company with the heart.

Through the music there is in him, the poet is enabled to make each natural thing utter the music there is in it. He is the enraptured spokesman of man and nature.

A good reader should have lights and shades in his voice, and what Sainte-Beuve calls insinuations.

Excellence in style depends primarily on clearness in thinking, and fineness of perception, this fineness implying some glow as well as health of sensibility.

Style goes beneath the surface: manner is superficial.

To write good poetry, the writer must have not only a good ear, but something very good to listen to internally.

The office of poetry is to set forth the best possibilities of the feelings. The poet is poet by having within him more of the finer life of feeling.

Sustained rapidity in poetry implies volume of thought, and thought so animated by feeling as to be urged ever fervently onward.

Naught is perfectly simple: every thing or thought is more or less combined, complicated, with others. The more intense the concentration of many in one, the more life and power; witness the similes and metaphors of Shakespeare.

The want of the sense of the ideal is a chief cause of the unprogressiveness of certain tribes and races.

The spontaneous has the highest quality. Foremost of human products is ranked a great Poem, the offspring of disinterested impulses and deep emotions, wrought into shape by intellect keen and clear.

Mannerism is a declension resulting from one-sidedness; but superior men are subject to it, because, although a defection from the purest style, it is a help to some who have more will than symmetry. It helps them with themselves, by allowing their faculties freer play, through the indulgence of their stronger inclinations, their disproportioned predominances of gift, which indulgence is the basis of mannerism; and, by thus giving more fluency and muscle to their movements, it helps them with readers. They write more and better than if, by a severer curb on their proclivities, they subdued their utterance to the clear quiet tone of simplicity. This is exemplified in Carlyle, and, in a finer way, in Tennyson.

Good poetry is the highest abstraction. The poet lives most in his mind; for a mark of his being a poet is, that his mind be lighted up with visions and imaginations, which draw him to them as his best company. On his brain his need of the beautiful is ever breeding fresh figures and conjunctions; and when these are vivid enough to take shape under the pen, he is abstracted from the earth and its forms, and swings up into an Empyrean of his own creating, where he moulds other forms, and, out of his thought, forges other realities and possibilities.

In some poetry there is too much individuality, and not enough universality.

In "Midsummer Night's Dream" it is as though in a calm summer night, standing on an eminence, were revealed to us by distant lightning, without noise, first in one quarter of the horizon, then in another, rich variegated scenery, every burst of glow laying bare a different landscape, each landscape vying with each for the palm of beauty.

The poet whose mind is become corrupt, as surely forfeits his creative birthright, as the rose its perfume through blight, or the fingers their cunning through palsy.

Is there not more poetry in Bacon's Essays in prose than in Pope's in verse? Pope said his say better in verse, because he had a metrical gift, a gift, be it said, very different from the rhythmic gift, and as inferior to that as talent is inferior to genius. This metrical gift helped to polish and condense his thoughts, besides giving them the benefit of measured cadence and the piquancy of rhyme. Men who have "the accomplishment of verse" in larger measure than poetic imagination, will, with a slight infusion of poetry, *seem* to be better poets than they are, being to the many acceptable from their very deficiency in the higher endowment, the major part of readers understanding and assimilating talent more readily than genius.

The dramatic claims to be the highest form

of poetry, because, that a drama be good, the poet must condense into small space characters that shall be life-like and poetic, at once individual and generic. Cardinal qualities of good dramatic poetry will be the liveliness, pointedness, rapidness, caused by interplay among individualities that are evoked, provoked, by contrasts and collisions, the wrestlings of talk and the rivalries of action, action giving to words, phrases, and rhythm, a brisk percussive movement. Without characterization there is no genuine drama: the evolution of character through close, frequent, diversified contacts, is the essence of dramatic as distinguished from lyric and epic treatment. But, besides sprightly individuality, springing, as it were, outward, there must be generalization, as profund as apt. Each personage, while distinct and individual, should be so thoroughly human as to be the easy mouthpiece of thoughts and sentiments that reach far. The weightier sentences will be unconsciously symbolical.

From the mind of Shakespeare, thoughts, sentiments, men, women leap forth, each into its right place, aglow with life, and motion, and grace; Shakespeare's brain is splendidly viviparous.

III.

CONDUCT, MANNERS.

PEOPLE in high places, who are not beneficent, are out of place.

In this "villainous world" there is almost as much unclean praise as malevolent censure.

To the opinions and creeds received from their fathers, men hold as to the houses and lands they have inherited. Spiritual and material they lump together, treating him who attacks their opinions like him who steals their cattle, not perceiving that, instead of a theft, the destruction of opinions is a barter, whereby they may gain a hundred fold. Thoughts are subject to higher laws than things.

In many an instance, when a man speaks of his conscience, conceit is mistaken for conscience.

By continuous breach of the moral law, men

forfeit mental growth. Napoleon and Cromwell grew not wiser as they grew older. Their minds did not ripen, they hardened.

Many of the old monasteries were founded by repentant reprobates; and the early sins of their founders bore, in many cases, fuller crops than their later virtues.

When a man readily gives ear to a slander, he betrays fellow-feeling with the malice whence it sprang.

We seek happiness by outwardly heaping on our puny selves all we can, each one building, with the joint force of his intellect and selfishness, a reversed pyramid, under the which the higher it rises, the more he is crushed on the small spot his small self can fill.

We are capable of life-long joy. Continuous varied fruition might be the sum of earthly existence. If our lives do not bring out this sum it is because we have misplaced, or mislaid, or overlooked, or misreckoned with, some of the counters.

"You cannot serve God and Mammon:" nay, you cannot serve yourself and Mammon.

The spokes of the wheel are helpless until bound together by the rim.

Christianity promises such moral splendors, that men, refusing to credit these as an earthly possibility, translate its consummations to the superearthly sphere. Priesthoods have always fostered this incredulity, which opens to them the imagination as their work-field, where tillage is much lighter than in a tangible soil. It is easier to saw air than to saw wood; easier to put the wretched off with sanctimonious assurances of celestial compensations, than to wrestle with earthly ills; easier to preach of Heaven to come than to abolish a present Hell. The conscientious pastor knows how almost fruitless a task it is, when, not content with stale ritual repetitions and wordy exhortations, he labors practically to purge and vivify his flock. With all his will and toil he brings little to pass. His theological tools are dull: what steel there was in them has worn off.   1852.

Children keep us at play all our lives.

Rich, inactive people, whose main business is the spending of money, lose their sense of the value of time, and lead a lethean life.

When we cease to learn, life loses its saltness.

Allopathy is monarchical and ecclesiastical, inasmuch as it looks to something out of the body to cure the body. Under the action of drugs the body is passive, only rousing itself against their disturbing or poisonous action. Hydropathy is democratic: the body must bestir itself for its own salvation. Self-reliant, it must use, for its protection and re-instatement, its native internal resources. Allopathy, acting from without, and by means of foreign substances, is one-sided, depressing, weakening: Hydropathy is all-sided, invigorating, purifying. Of a human body weighing one hundred and fifty pounds, one hundred pounds are pure water; hence the efficacy of water as a curative agent.

Idleness is the root of most evil; and the minds that are busy to keep other minds idle, are doing the basest work that men can do.

Give me the man who will not desert himself.

A human being can only be developed by work. He who will not work fails to fulfill his manhood: he who cannot work is less than a man.

There is a logic in everything. The best knowledge is that by which this logic is mastered.

Among our American rights is not the right of ignorance; for ignorance is an absolute obstacle to self-government. To keep our track clear of this grossest obstruction, individual means are insufficient. For its own weal's sake, for its life's sake, the State must work actively against ignorance.

A lie is the most hateful of things. We say, As true as the Sun. A lie is an eclipse of light. Were all people to lie, we should be shrouded in a moral darkness blacker than a starless and moonless midnight.

Allowing for imaginative amplification, still

the chivalrous protection of women in the thirteenth and fourteenth centuries denotes a vast enlargement of humanity at that period, and, like all manifestations from the depths of human feeling, is a splendid promise sure to be fulfilled.

Never did the greatness of a cause, or of ideas, or of principles, lift Napoleon above himself. He was never inspired.

The union of many weak threads makes a strong rope; but the union of many fools begets not wisdom, but only worse folly.

Lafayette was not a great man, but he was a man of great friendships. He was the friend of struggling America, the friend of freedom, and the friend of Washington.

The Greek for man is *anthropos*, which means looker up.

The human mind is so constituted that it must busy itself much with small things. If wholesome details are not within its reach, it will resort to frivolities, gossip, worldly pettiness. Give it productive attractive work, in and with nature, and you forestall empty officiousness, unprofitable busy-ness, morbid self-gnawing.

Few minds are capable of broad generalization. Of prominent public men not one in ten has a comprehensive grasp and innate room for expansion. High places are mostly attained, not through mental superiority, but through impudence, activity, and talent for pushing.

Love kindles love: hate engenders hate.

Work is a tie between man and nature: it should be a bond of brotherhood among men. Through heartless unmitigated competition it is a source of envies, jealousies, hates.

If a man shuts his religion up in a pew, or keeps it as a solitary solace, which sheds hardly a ray on others, he hides his light, not under a bushel, but under the smoke and ashes of a barren egotism.

Whenever there is a deep disturbance and

broad displacement among the elements of any large whole, there will be violent explosive convulsions, in order to restore the equilibrium needed for health and even for life. Such disturbances imply strong organic vitality in the constituents. To this deep general perturbation, a people incapable of long development and high culture will not be subject, its elements not being quick and various enough for large and pervasive breach of equilibrium. But for a great progressive people, ascending or already ascended, to a high civilization, equilibrium can only be restored by an English rebellion of 1640, or a French Revolution, or an American civil war.

So many men there are about whom the most interesting thing to other people is their last will and testament.

The child is not only father to the man, but brother, too, most men in mature years approving themselves childish. Their natures not having ripened and deepened with years, they continue to be willful and passion-governed, much busied with trifles, exhibiting an infantile tenaciousness for their petty pretensions, an unreasoning persistence in narrow opinions, an unabated interest in the ephemeral.

The basis of coöperative success is sympathy. The conditions of wise associative work insure progress and purification.

The soul, being endued with a beautiful body, seeks to improve the body by dress and adornment, which may be looked upon as a continuance of the soul's incarnation. This is a transcendental excuse for the time and pains women give to the arts of the toilet.

"It has been noted," says Lord Bacon, "that those who ascribe openly too much to their own wisdom and policy, end unfortunate." A good epigraph for an essay on self-conceit.

History abundantly proves that priesthoods exhibit supreme unscrupulousness, audacity, impiety; unique invention in torture and murder; utter undutifulness and shamelessness in their means to gain and keep power; the coldest selfishness; unfailing readiness to subject the spiritual to the carnal, from motives of greed or ambition.

The best men of "society" have all travelled; if not geographically, at least they have been far, and have learnt much from converse with all sorts of people, and from study of the deepest and wisest pages.

Men cling to the past, not because it is old, but because it is part of themselves. They live under and sleep under it, as under a roof that belongs to them. It becomes a form of that Proteus, selfishness. Nothing is more egotistic than stiff conservatism.

Among some of the cultivated heads in America there prevails a spiritual egotism, whereby, instead of referring all things and beings (themselves included) up to God, they would draw God down to them, and would imbue Him with themselves. It is the *reductio ad absurdum* of individualism, subjectivity delirious; and it sways at times even sober sane men. Believing themselves to move under upright motives, some are inly demoralized (just as Robespierre was) by a self-estimation so intense as to be unconscious, impelling them to make their own thought and will supreme. When it happens that one of these is justly conscious of not being sordid or greedy or vulgarly ambitious, he is driven to still greater extremes by this very consciousness, which, through the subtle yeast of egotism, becomes the fomenter of only a deeper selfishness. He will push his theories and convictions into practice at whatever cost. One proof of the vice in the extreme principles of such men (and it is overwhelming proof) is, that in pursuing their ends they exhibit more hate than love.

More people are kept from injustice by prudence than by principle.

Taking medicine is another form of the weakness that makes us look out of ourselves for help.

By some who would weigh Washington his nobility of nature is overlooked ; and some do not give prominence to his integrity and largeness of soul. I have read one attempt to characterize Washington by a writer who thinks his chief quality was constancy !

If you wish to mark your contempt for a man, tell him a lie.

Introverted attention, referring to self all that is said, inattentiveness from want of sympathy, causing indifference of manner, these are signs of habitual inward self-engrossment, outwardly exhibited in bad manners, which have their chief source in too much self-regard and not enough regard for others, too much inlook and not enough outlook. Good manners are objective: many people are not only too subjective, but narrowly, churlishly subjective.

To make a "good society" are wanted people, and a good many of them, who live, not upon their money, but upon their minds; not even upon the money their minds may earn.

The Egyptians used to call a library "the remedy for diseases of the soul."

The larger and richer a nature is, the more objective it is; that is, the more easily and fully are its sympathies enlisted for objects and beings beyond itself, and the more clearly can it see what is outside of itself. There is to a fly no *objective*, except where his feet stand or his mouth sucks. Exclusive subjectivity is egotism strung to intenseness. We are all too much contracted and heaped up into ourselves, having, as Montaigne says, our sight shortened to the length of our noses.

All society, whatever its form, rests on work, grows out of work.

The victim of envy is not the envi*ee*, but the envi*er*.

In many men there is no echo to one who speaks wisely; in some from want of thought, in some from want of the right kind or degree of feeling.

In the personality of a man we take a loving interest, in proportion as in his doings or his writings he has expanded beyond himself into acts and thoughts of cordial value.

We are ever interposing and obtruding ourselves between us and our good.

To manners, as to literature, grace is a quality needed to complete them. Grace is from within.

If men would but be upright and fearless. Fear not, and work on at thy mental enlargement, trusting to the Most High. Above all, fear not. He who fears is possessed with a devil, and a mean devil.

Man is distinguished from animals by foresight, and man from man by foresight. All wrong, injustice, selfishness, is shortsighted.

The worldly gentleman is apt to wear a coat of coldness, woven from within.

Detractors are great levelers, downwards.

In some people what is called manners is an excess of manner.

Proportion is a mighty power. Onesidedness makes and keeps many people wrong in regard to great principles.

Good intellectual faculties give sight: nothing but sensibility gives insight.

So many able men are always seeking themselves and not the truth.

Is not Guizot's a rather shallow hard head?

Life has many deep, rich rhythms which are as yet only heard by a few, through a rare inward hearing.

Wishes, desires, that we ought not to gratify, we can turn to account for our good, if we will arrest their hurtful outward flow, and, by controlling, make of them sources of inward fortification.

In the long run everything depends upon the self. The inward of a man must be active and coöperative, in order that the best opportunities be profited by, that the most prosperous circumstances be not baffled or wasted.

The spirit of Christian charity, of brotherly respect, is finely exhibited and characteristically expressed in the following passage of a letter from Goethe to Lavater. Sentences like these are often met with in Goethe, and make one think of him as a higher Franklin. " Most thankful should we be that into every living being Nature has put so much healing power, that when there is a lesion anywhere it can knit itself together again; and what are our thousandfold religions other than thousand-formed manifestations of this inward healing power? My plaster does not suit thee, nor thine me: In our Father's apotheca are many recipes. So I have nothing to answer to your letter, nothing to contradict in it: but on the other hand much to place beside it. We should put our confessions of faith side by side in two columns, and thereupon build a bond of peace and tolerance."

Especially in regard to the relations of the sexes, people will one of these days be in all their inward motions and outward doings as virtuous as a dressy congregation looks when it has just seated itself, some spring Sunday, in a carpeted pew-cushioned church that has a richly-paid rector.

A man who has a sense of the ideal carries about with him an hourly educator.

IV.

MISCELLANEOUS.

The mummies of Egypt are a type of unenlightened conservatism, — a childish effort to perpetuate corporeal bulk, to eternize the perishable, to subordinate essence to form, to deny death. The result is a mummy.

Hereditary oligarchs are puppets to whom motion is imparted by wires inserted under ground into the dead bodies of their forefathers.

The remedy for England is to turn, not her waste lands to use, but her waste mind, her waste intellect and feeling. This, her priceless, inexhaustible domain, is half tilled in patches.

In England so many people look as though they were waiting for my lord.

On the continent of Europe it looks as

though government had been made first, and man afterwards.

The great recent discoveries of Gall, of Fourier, of Priesnitz, all combine to make apparent the resources, the incalculable vigors, the inborn capabilities of man.

Forms soon usurp upon the substance they were designed to hold. Ceremony and hypocritical corporeal salutations get to be a substitute for genuine politeness; religion is smothered under ritual observances; paper money drives out metal, which it was devised to represent.

The Greeks and the English seem to be the only two nations possessing enough sap and vigor and fullness of nature to reproduce themselves in distant soils, through colonists that swarmed off from the parent hive.

Cherished should be the man whose mind is too large to be filled by creeds, and too manly to close itself against any wants of humanity. The mental home of the truest men is among principles, and principles are infinitely expansive.

People nominally worship God one day in the week, and really worship Mammon seven.

The Bible should be studied with activity of spirit. Its great heart will not beat but to the throbbing of yours. Just to read it passively, traditionally, dulls the very susceptibility through which it is to be taken in. Not thus will you find God in the Bible. Who has not first sought Him in his own heart and in the life around him, will scarcely find Him there at all. God is not locked up in the Bible: He is at all times around, within us. Strive with Jesus to feel his presence. Then you may hope for promotion, purification, inspiration: then your heart may bring forth biblical chapters; for, the best there is in the Bible came out of the human soul, touched to inspired utterances by the awakened inward divinity.

The priests of Rome discourage intercourse with God through the Bible, which is already at one remove. Themselves they constitute the sole interpreters of the divine. The heavenly will can only be expressed by distillation through the foul alembics of priestly greeds and ambition. Hence, where they long dominate, religion becomes materialized, and, for uplifting, soul-purging communion with God, is substituted abject, demoralizing, belittling submission to priesthood.

An ape is a creature that has approached the gates of reason, and stands there grinning and jabbering in tragi-comical ignorance of his nearness to the regal palace.

Envy, like venomous reptiles, can only strike at short distances.

There is no deeper law of nature than that of change.

Everything that we do being a cause, he is the most sagacious who so does that each cause shall have its good effect. This practical long-sightedness is wisdom, the want of it foolishness. To-days are all fathers of to-morrows, but like many other fathers, they sadly neglect their paternal duties. To-day, if it thinks at all, thinks of itself, and leaves to-morrow to shift for itself. Life is a daily laying of eggs, some to be hatched to-morrow, some next month, some next year, some next century.

Many are not hatched at all, but rot or are broken; many come prematurely out of the shell, and perish from debility; and thus that much life is wasted. Charity is long-sighted, selfishness is short-sighted. And yet, so defective is our social constitution, that a man may be long-sighted in using his neighbor for his own ends. Thus doctors — who are short-sighted when they take their own physic, which they seldom do — are long-sighted when they give it to their patients; for the more of it these take, the oftener the doctor is called. It were a mistake to suppose that parsons are long-sighted because they set their minds so much upon the next world; their long-sightedness consists in directing other people's thoughts to that quarter, while from the supermundane spectators they draw the wherewithal to be content with this. Lawyers are short-sighted when they encourage litigation; the long-sighted know that the perverted passions of civilized men will bring grist enough to their mill without their stir. The man who sells rum is short-sighted, but less so than he who drinks it. Authors are very short-sighted when they write to please the public, instead of writing to please the truth. Expedients are short-sighted, principles long-sighted; and notwithstanding the apparent prosperity of some liars, nothing is so long-sighted as truth.

We Americans let not the past accumulate upon us: we make clean work as we go. We keep the present lively, because we are ever snatching a new present from across the confines of the future. We are always "going ahead;" that is, building up the future out of itself and not solely out of the past. We don't wait for the future: we rush in pursuit of it.

Classification is the highest function of intellect; it brings order out of chaos. It is both analysis and synthesis. The higher the department of universal life, the keener of course must be the intellectual insight that can detect its organic law. To order minerals is feebler work than to order morals. The man who classes, needs to have a kind of creative mastery over his material. He intellectually recreates. The savage, who has mastery over nothing, but is a serf of Nature, has no power of classification.

To weave the wondrous form wherewith life

invests itself in humanity, the heart works ceaselessly, and every organ, member, part and particle of the living frame works, each joyfully in its sphere, in unison with the heart, for the maintenance of the common fabric. But a continuation and extension of the unconscious work of the heart and lungs is the conscious work of the head and hand of man, whose end is, to feed, to clothe, to lodge, to develop, to delight his body and his mind. All work, the unconscious and the conscious, is but life methodized, that is, life made more living, more intelligent, and thence more productive. And thus work, which is the condition and result of life, becomes the means of its perpetuation, its extension, its elevation. All work may be delightful; and as, the healthier the body is, the more joyfully and thoroughly the heart and its allies perform their unconscious task, so in a healthy social organization all work, the greatest and the least, ceasing to be repulsive and becoming attractive and delightful, would be proportionately productive. A consummation this, not barely, most devoutly to be wished, but most surely to be accomplished, by that high work which the intellect exalted by love and faith is equal to performing.

Nature rejects with contempt hereditary aristocracy.

In our present misorganized society helplessness is the condition, not of nine in ten, but of all. The wisest and wealthiest are encompassed by exposure, dangers, calamity. The most of what is done on earth is of our own making or allowing. Heaven is just, lets us do for our good or ill, and helps us when we help ourselves. Put we our shoulders to the wheel, the Hercules is instantly at our side. We make the beds we lie in; not you *or* I, but you *and* I, and all the you's and I's that surround us. Against our needs and woes you *or* I can do little, but you *and* I everything. Association, which has made banks and railroads, can do much better and higher.

There is nothing that some people are more ignorant of than their own ignorance.

Unsightly is an old face haunted by the vices of youth.

Credulity is a characteristic of weakness. Imagination precedes Reason. Fancies are a loose substitute for knowledge. Hence the unreasonable creeds of young nations, fastened upon them by priestcraft, whose criminal practice it has been, and is still, by terrifying the imagination to subjugate the reason. The first-born of priestcraft was the Devil.

Priests are ever shuffling over the leaves of old books: they seek God in traditions and hearsays, and the dim utterances of the livers of old; they abide by the outgivings of obsolete mystics: they re-assert the beliefs of antiquated seers: they grovel and grope in the darkness and dawn, to find stakes planted by the crude beginners of the world, to which, by grossest cords, they would bind to the past our forward-reaching souls. The future, too, they suborn and would monopolize. Out of imaginations that are shallow, unhallowed, meagre, foul, they would construct both the past and the future. That they may be paid for furnishing rush-lights, they cultivate darkness, and becurtain with creeds and dogmas the human tabernacle against the sun of truth. Those who appeal to the God of light, and to the upright soul of man, against their sophistications, and usurpations, they crucify. Audaciously they dub themselves the ministers of God, they who are especially not God's ministers but men's. Spiritual insight, moral elevation, rich sympathies, these are the tokens whereby the divinely ordained are signalized. Are candidates for any priesthood admitted or rejected by these signs? Not by inborn superiorities of sensibility, but by acquired proficiencies, by intellectual adoptions are they tested. This creed, these articles, this ritual, — do they accept these, then are they accepted. To be learned in humanity, a vivid learning, which the large heart imbibes without labor, this is not their title; but to be learned in theology, a lifeless learning, which the small head can acquire by methodical effort. They would live and make others live by the dead letter, and not by the living law. The dead letter is the carcass of what has been, or what is imagined to have been. The living law is what is: it is not written, it is forever in process of being written, on the heart of man by the hand of God.

Disproportion is disqualification. Too much is unwieldy: too little is feebleness. A giant is of no more use than a dwarf. A man seven feet high finds his extra foot a daily incumbrance. A man of more head than heart is dangerous: a man of more heart than head is a victim.

In one of the "Latter Day Pamphlets," Mr. Carlyle asks tauntingly, What have the Americans done? — We have abolished Monarchy; we have abolished hereditary Oligarchy; we have sundered Church and State; we have so wrought with our English inheritance, that most Englishmen better their condition by quitting the old home and coming to the new. We have consolidated a State, under whose disinterested guardianship the cabined and straitened of the Old World find enlargement and prosperity. We have suppressed standing armies; we have decentralized government to an extent that, before our experiment, was deemed hopeless; we have grown with such dream-like rapidity, as to stand, after little more than a half-century of national existence, prominent on the earth among the nations; and this, in large measure, through the wisdom of political organization, whereby such scope is given to industry and invention, that not only are our native means profitably developed, but the great influx of Europeans is healthfully absorbed. We have in seventy years put between the Atlantic and the Pacific an Empire of twenty-five millions, who work more than any twenty-five millions on earth, and read more than any other fifty millions. We have built a State at once so solid and flexible, that it protects all without oppressing any. Our land is a hope and a refuge to the king-crushed laborers of Europe, and from the eminence above all other lands to which it has ascended, by our forecast, vigor, and freedom, it is to the thinker a demonstration of the upward movement of Christendom, and a justification of hopes that look to still higher elevations.

Mr. Carlyle's sneers at our lack of heroism would be unworthy of him, from their very silliness, were they not more so from their sour injustice. Let any People recite its heroic deeds, on flood or field, since we were a nation, and we will match every one of them. And in the private sphere, where self-sacrifice, devotion, courage, find such scope for heroic virtues, our social life is warm with them: but this is no theme for words. For his unworthy ones, we deem well enough of Mr. Carlyle to believe, that, when disengaged from the morbidly subjective, and therefore blinding and demoralizing, moods, to which he is liable, he is ashamed of having printed them. It looks somewhat as though this passage had been written just to give us an opportunity of victorious retort, or to tempt us into an exhibition of our national propensity to brag, — a propensity, be it said, which is national in every nation we know anything of, whether English, French, German, or Italian. We only beat them in bragging, just as we beat them in ploughs and statues, in clippers and steamboats, in whalemen and electric telegraphs, in cheap newspapers and cheap government. They all do their best at bragging, and so do we, — and we beat them. 1852.

The moral world is better lighted than heretofore. Selfishness succeeds somewhat less grossly: conscience has a louder voice.

Such is the power of relative proportion that the same chemical atoms, commingled in different ratios, give substances of most diverse natures. Of men the same holds good, and in a still higher degree.

The truer religion is the simpler and more

silent it is; but simplicity and silence suit not priestcraft.

Never make pretentions which you cannot justify. Therefore never strive to seem young when you are not young: time will expose you to daily mortification. Time is vital to us: by trying to live against time we maim ourselves.

The lawyer is retrospective: his masters are behind him: the authority of the past controls him: his studies are of the decisions of dead men and their interpretations of other dead men's ordinances. Thus his mind is apt to become inclosed within conventional juridical bounds. Hence lawyers are seldom great statesmen, the function of the statesman being, to grasp large present relations. The lawyer's domain is chiefly what has been: the statesman's what is, and what is to be.

Man is of the vine nature: he puts forth tendrils that need props and supports in his fellow-men: and, failing these, he misses his altitude and proper prosperity, and droops and creeps.

When with thoughtful watchfulness we study creation and its processes, we find true the remark of Playfair, "How much further reason may sometimes go than imagination can venture to follow."

The "cloth" of the clergy is too often cut into a cloak.

Life is a universal boundless whole, whereof each one as a part is valuable in proportion to the quality of his relations to the whole.

Satire implies a high state already attained and a higher attainable. Humanity is never satirized in its lower conditions.

Between truth and freedom there is a close interdependence and union. Jean Paul says that to romance (or to lie) is derived from Roman, the word with this signification having come into use after the Romans had become enslaved.

In air made foul by human exhalations, a material filth penetrates to the finest fibres of the brain, weakening and impeding the mind's action. The difference between the "black hole of Calcutta" and many of our school-rooms is this: in the black hole scores died in a few hours: from the school-rooms hundreds go forth to die in a few years, from effects of the same cause. A building, especially a public one which is liable to crowds, should be a breathing organism, ever, like the lungs, throwing out used air and drawing in fresh.

Present intuitions of genial deep-thoughted men, even of the deepest, are in part a fruit of past intuitions, culture generating an atmosphere whereon the largest brains are unconsciously fed.

In the frenzied heat of brain-fever France engendered Marat and Robespierre, deformed monsters of self-sufficiency, whom in her delirium she hugged as comely healthy children.

Some people are practically honest from reverence for property. They will sin against you or me, against truth, against the Holy Ghost, but not against property.

Napoleon was a colossal torso.

From one of the pages of Lacordaire's "Conférences de Toulouse," I copy this tremendous sentence: "Mahomet, initié à l'Evangile, a revêtu de chair la félicité souveraine; et ce fantôme de son Paradis persécute encore la honteuse imagination de ses croyants, seul peuple qui n'ait pas connu la pudeur."

Reason should always hold the reins of the mind. If they are loosely held, the mind stumbles, or runs off the track, or runs away.

We speak of "here and hereafter;" but man's life is an everpresent here, an everlasting now. The hereafter is ever turning into *here:* the future is forever becoming *now*.

Few men have the kind and degree of mental vitality needed to throb with the life-currents which slake and vivify the organism. The minds of most men being rather mechanical and material than dynamic and psychical, to them the human organism is too much a mechanism. Medical practitioners work by rule and routine more than by insight and law. They can analyze the dead blood: they cannot track the pulsing life-stream Few of them fully apprehend the plastic power of nature; and hence they so often pull down where they should build up, mutilate or destroy where they should save.

The next generation will have to reverse the accustomed phrase at the beginning of many biographies, and say, " His parents, *though rich*, were honest."

The universally innate human religious aptitude was in the Semitic people intensified by the aridity of part of their soil and the neighborhood of vast deserts. By the daily maleficent presence of these, their helplessness and their dependence on the unseen were brought fearfully home to them, and incessantly. From the want of resources and of breadth in their territory there was among them an enforced simplicity of earthly occupations, which left them leisure, and gave them disposition, to fill their minds with thoughts of the power that seemed to press on them in the desert and to stint them in their fields and streams. Thence their notion of Deity was more of might than of beneficence. Their God was a God of anger rather than of love. Their conception of a life beyond the grave was null, or faint.

There are people in whom the best thing is their appetite for dinner.

Equality before the law, man-made law, is one of the great conquests of latter times, — a conquest bearing in its train inestimable profits. A relative equality is this, equal rights in presence of all human tribunals ; and such impartiality is a prerequisite for full liberty. But absolute equality is an absurdity, and men's attempt to establish it is destructive of free development and free use of faculties developed, a revolt against nature involving tyranny over man. Men are born with unequal gifts, moral as well as intellectual, and this inequality involves vast consequences, personal, political, and social. Moreover, the wider the range of this inequality, the better the materials for a solid and attractive and elastic social structure.

To show man's innate capacity of goodness, to exhibit him as born of God and not a cross between God and the Devil (as he is represented by what is called Christian theology), this is a task for the present and coming generations.

Providence is large in its designs, and uses minute instruments. Common statesmanship is small in its designs, and uses large means for shallow plans.

When you talk to a Romish priest and, in a less degree, to a Protestant clergyman, you feel that you are talking, not to a self-directed individual man, to a whole human being, but to the fraction of a partial sum of men, to a bit of a segment of a limited circle, to the cog of a wheel, whose action is circumscribed and defined by its position. And is not this the case when talking to most men, lay as well as clerical? Few but are mere fragments of humanity, cabined in set opinions, tethered to inexorable creeds and constitutions.

The Puritans were a one-sided race, and that one side was much on the side of self. Yet, in modern development, what a great and indispensable part they played.

The man who cannot learn new thoughts becomes stagnant. If he lives in a progressive community he is left uncomfortably behind, he and his. The generations that stride forward walk past him or over him. Thus it was with the French *noblesse* after 1789; and so it is now with "old families" that will not learn. In these electric times they are thrust from their thrones by families that have aptitude for new things. An old race that cannot take in new principles thereby shows that it is exhausted, is become mentally barren. Witness China, and the East generally.

The life of man on earth is but a beginning; and beginnings are tentative, crude, imperfect. Hence, blunders, vices, crimes; and hence, men being so frail and shortsighted, so many bad men are allowed to get into high places.

Is not the addiction to rites and cermonies, the attaching of essential importance to forms, a sign of the want of sensibility? An inward vacancy manifests itself in an outward ostentation.

Noteworthy is it how our civilization is built on piles, so to speak, resting so much on human imaginations and ordonnances, on ecclesiastical dogmas and legislative enactments. Out of a crude natural state man rises gradually into a cultivated artificial state. Out of this, too, he will pass, and through self-projections and emancipations reach the ripe natural state, where dogmatic theology and jurisprudence and all makeshifts will have been outgrown, and humanity will securely rest on the God-given law.

The imagination is the truest of mental powers. It reveals to us our inmost self; and so truly, that we dare not make known all its promptings and pictures.

Dreary and dark is the outlook of the materialist: closed is his mind against the light and warmth of higher spheres, which potentially belong to mankind: to him there come, from the unknown vast, no flashes too brilliant to be borne, save for a moment, by earthly man, hinting at and prefiguring radiant trans-earthly possibilities. When in "Achilleis" Goethe describes the Hours as lavishing upon and within the abode of Jupiter "so much light and life that man could not have borne it, but the gods it delighted," he depicts the life of a higher state of being, which low-thoughted materialism will not entertain, but something of which there must have been at all times many to conceive, or man would have groped forever in the caves of savagery. Had man not been the subject of restless spiritual up-reachings, of instinctive heavenward aspirations, no philosophical plane could ever have been reached; and thence, no materialist would have gained the culture which enables him to strive to span the universe with his tape-line of phenomenal sequences, to seize the mystery of being through chemical manipulations, to weigh the essences of life in grocer's scales.

In 1456 Pope Calixtus III. issued a bull against a comet. The absurd impotence of this proceeding was some antidote to its blasphemous venom. The four centuries that, since the day of impious Calixtus, have rolled themselves out of the bosom of eternity, sparkling more and more with the divine light of poetic and scientific revelation, have left unhealed, untouched, the presumptuous vision of the Papacy. Its bad distinction is that it will not, cannot, be enlightened. In Nature, in Civilization, in Christendom, it stands alone in stolid unchangeableness, self-exiled from the Paradise of progression by ecclesiastical ambition, by self-worshipping loneliness. As blasphemous to day as in the age of Calixtus, it looks upon every free-thinking; free-speaking mind as a cometary intrusion, a menacing irregularity, a defiant insolence, whose light and being it would, if it could, extinguish by a bull; in its arrogant irreverence blind to the deep religious fact, that every such mind is launched by the same infinite Might that projects comets and places the stars. How many Protestants are there who denounce Popery, and yet practice its blasphemy against free thought and free speech?

In every department of work the highest achievement implies the organizing, coördinating power. Without it a man can hardly be great, whether he be scientist, statesman, or poet.

The power of capital lies in the intelligence which creates and preserves it.

The minds of many people are so imprisoned in narrow, false theologies that they look out upon the world as a convict does through his prison-bars.

So many men are afraid of God ! Most tragic condition ! They stick to the old man-made, miry, thoroughfares, too timid to strike into the God-given paths that open on all sides, smiling and glittering with safe solicitations, with promises as brilliant as sure. Disabled, hectic theologies they prefer to science, contracted dogma to expanded reason. More pitiable are they than monkeys, who stand senselessly chattering before the temple of Thought and Speech, and have no power to enter.

The men who, lacking the insight which comes chiefly from sympathy, are by nature incompetent to grasp and appreciate the profound principles and springs of life and motion that underlie and energize all being, especially human being, these are the men who put themselves forward to read and interpret the secrets and the will of the prime Motor, men for the most part as limited in intellectual range as in sensibility.

One thing keeps fresh a day, another a month, another a year, another a century, another a thousand years : truth, justice, love, keep themselves forever fresh.

A man cannot better spend his life than in learning how to live.

Oriental despotism dominating the law and ritual of the Jews, minute directions were prescribed for all individual doings, compressing, smothering personal liberty and self-direction The tendency of the spiritual teaching of Jesus was to emancipate men from this priestly domination and interference.

There should be no hostility between theology and science ; for theology, or knowledge of the ways and will of God, should be, and, if sound, will be and must be, founded on science; that is, on sifted, methodized knowledge.

Violent death is a proof of incompleteness, of failure. Two men or two armies, destroying one another, show that man is not yet out of the phase of animalism, and needs farther purging through swift destruction.

Human society is founded on sensualism ; sensualism in a healthy sense. The structure is weakened, or threatened, or deformed, when the foundations obtrude above the ground.

Water is more strengthening than whiskey, more exhilarating than wine.

Every dollar of capital extant is the product of work, work of muscle and work of mind; and a part of the function of capital, its chief part, should be, to react upon the mind and muscle of a community, for the profit, improvement, and elevation of all its members. The material is the creation of the spiritual, and should serve its maker.

No new thing under the sun! Everything under the sun is new, except what is dying or dead; and death itself is but a passage to a new condition of life. Whatever has life renews itself momently: when it ceases to renew itself, it is losing its present form of being. Constant renewal is the very life of being. Every sunrise is new, every soul is a new soul. Because all men and things are alike, each is therefore not the less new: no two among the myriads that are and have been are precisely alike, and this infinitude of unlikeness is a token of the newness of each. Here is exhibited the boundless prodigality of materials and resources at command of the sleepless productiveness in the animating principle. "Behold, I make all things new." Timoleon was a new man: Are William the Silent of Orange and Washington, because they bear strong likeness to Timoleon, less lustrously new? Was not Patrick Henry a new orator? Was not Shelley a new poet? Unceasing creativeness is the very essence of the originating, sustaining, informing, Mind. Hence the daily, hourly rejuvenation of the earth, and all that is on it, by the pauseless pulse of the Eternal Soul.

THE END.